The Egyptian Hieroglyph Metaphysical Language

Moustafa Gadalla

Tehuti Research Foundation
International Head Office: Greensboro, NC, U.S.A.

The Egyptian Hieroglyph
Metaphysical Language
by Moustafa Gadalla

Published by:
Tehuti Research Foundation
P.O. Box 39491
Greensboro, NC 27438, U.S.A.

All rights reserved. No part of this book may be reproduced or transmitted in any form or by any means, electronic or mechanical, including photocopying, recorded or by any information storage and retrieval system without written permission from the author, except for the inclusion of brief quotations in a review.

Copyright © 2016 and 2018 by Moustafa Gadalla, All rights reserved.

Publisher's Cataloging-in-Publication Data

Gadalla, Moustafa, 1944-
The Egyptian Hieroglyph Metaphysical Language / Moustafa Gadalla.
p. cm.
Includes bibliographical references.

Library of Congress Control Number: 2016900014
ISBN-13(pdf): 978-1-931446-95-2
ISBN-13(e-book): 978-1-931446-96-9
ISBN-13(pbk.): 978-1-931446-97-6

1.Egyptian language. 2. Cosmology, Egyptian. 3. Egypt–Religion. 4. Occultism–Egypt 5. Egypt–Civilization. 6. Egypt–History–To 640 A.D. I. Title.

Updated 2018

CONTENTS

About the Author   vii
Preface   viii
Standards and Terminology   xi
Map of Ancient Egypt   xiii

Chapter 1 : Historical Deception of the (Ancient) Egyptian Linguistics   1

1.1 The Imagery and Alphabetical Writing Modes   1
1.2 The Universal Pictorial Signs   3
1.3 The Egyptian Pictorial Metaphysical Images/ Script   4

Chapter 2 : The Scientific/Metaphysical Realities of Pictorial Images   8

2.1 Images: Language of the Mind/ Consciousness/Divine   8
2.2 The Soundness of the Three Roles of Each Egyptian Hieroglyphic Image   10
2.3 The Interpretation Process of Serial Images in the Consciousness   15

Chapter 3 : Egyptian Hieroglyphic Imagery Depiction of Thoughts	22
3.1 Ideograms of Ideas [Images as Metaphysical Symbols]	22
3.2 An Overview of the Egyptian Formation of Ideograms	24
Chapter 4 : Animal Hieroglyphic Images	29
4.1 Metaphysical Significance of Animal Images	29
4.2 Sample Related Egyptian Hieroglyphic Images	30
Chapter 5 : Human and Animal-Headed Human Hieroglyphic Images	59
5.1 Metaphysical Significance of Human Images	59
5.2 Metaphysical Significance of Animal Headed Images	59
5.3 Sample Related Egyptian Hieroglyphic Images	60
Chapter 6 : Human Body Parts Hieroglyphic Images	64
6.1 Metaphysical Significance of Human Body Parts Images	64
6.2 Sample Related Egyptian Hieroglyphic Images	66
Chapter 7 : Nature and Geometrical Figure Hieroglyphic Images	77
7.1 Sample Related Egyptian Hieroglyphic Images	77
Chapter 8 : Man Made Object Hieroglyphic Images	89
8.1 Metaphysical Significance of Man Made Objects Images	89
8.2 Sample Related Egyptian Hieroglyphic Images	90

Selected Bibliography	97
Sources and Notes	101
TRF Publications	111

ABOUT THE AUTHOR

Moustafa Gadalla is an Egyptian-American independent Egyptologist who was born in Cairo, Egypt in 1944. He holds a Bachelor of Science degree in civil engineering from Cairo University.

Gadalla is the author of twenty-two published, internationally acclaimed books about various aspects of the Ancient Egyptian history and civilization and its influences worldwide.

He is the Founder and Chairman of the Tehuti Research Foundation (**https://www.egypt-tehuti.org**)—an international, U.S.-based nonprofit organization dedicated to Ancient Egyptian studies. He is also the Founder and Head of the online Egyptian Mystical University (**https://www.EgyptianMysticalUniversity.org**).

From his early childhood, Gadalla pursued his Ancient Egyptian roots with passion, through continuous study and research. Since 1990, he has dedicated and concentrated all his time to researching and writing.

PREFACE

A picture is worth a 1,000 words. A picture represents a concept/idea and not a single letter/sound.

We say "picture this" or "imagine that" for images are representations of concepts and ideas beyond words. The picture conveys information more efficiently than letters/words.

This book covers the Egyptian Hieroglyph metaphysical language of images/pictures, which is the language of the mind/intellect/divine.

It is the aim of this book to provide such an exposition; one which, while based on sound scholarship, will present the issues in language comprehensible to non-specialist readers. Technical terms have been kept to a minimum.

This book is divided into 8 chapters.

Chapter 1: *Historical Deception of the (Ancient) Egyptian Linguistics* will clear the confusion intended to misrepresent the Egyptian hieroglyphics as a primitive form of writing with individual sound values. The Egyptian Hieroglyphics are ideograms which are different and they have nothing to do with the Egyptian alphabetical system.

Chapter 2: *The Scientific/Metaphysical Realities of Pictorial Images (Hieroglyphs)* explains how human beings process information received from the five senses to the brain through visualized images; how each hieroglyphic image has imitative and symbolic (figurative and allegorical) meanings; the concurrence in modern science of such multiple meanings of each image; and how a series of images are processed in the consciousness the same way, like a dream is processed.

Chapter 3: *Egyptian Hieroglyphic Imagery Depictions of Thoughts* explains how Egyptian hieroglyphic images represent metaphysical concepts; relationships between their functions and geometrical forms; and provides an overview of the Egyptian formation of such ideograms.

Chapter 4: *Animal Hieroglyphic Images* explains the metaphysical significance of such images and highlights the significance of over 30 related Egyptian Hieroglyphic images.

Chapter 5: *Human and Animal-headed Human Hieroglyphic Images* explains the metaphysical significance of such images and highlights the significance of about 10 related Egyptian Hieroglyphic images.

Chapter 6: *Human Body Parts Hieroglyphic Images* explains the metaphysical significance of such images and highlights the significance of over 10 related Egyptian Hieroglyphic images.

Chapter 7: *Nature and Geometrical Figure Hieroglyphic Images* explains the metaphysical significance of such images and highlights the significance of over 10 related Egyptian Hieroglyphic images.

Chapter 8: *Man Made Object Hieroglyphic Images* explains the metaphysical significance of such images and highlights the significance of about 20 related Egyptian Hieroglyphic images.

Moustafa Gadalla

STANDARDS AND TERMINOLOGY

1. The Ancient Egyptian word neter and its feminine form netert have been wrongly, and possibly intentionally, translated to 'god' and 'goddess' by almost all academics. Neteru (the plural of neter/netert) are the divine principles and functions of the One Supreme God.

2. You may find variations in writing the same Ancient Egyptian term, such as Amen/Amon/Amun or Pir/Per. This is because the vowels you see in translated Egyptian texts are only approximations of sounds which are used by Western Egyptologists to help them pronounce the Ancient Egyptian terms/words.

3. We will be using the most commonly recognized words for the English-speaking people that identify a neter/netert [god, goddess], a pharaoh, or a city; followed by other 'variations' of such a word/term.

It should be noted that the real names of the deities (gods, goddesses) were kept secret so as to guard the cosmic power of the deity. The Neteru were referred to by epithets that describe particular qualities, attributes and/or aspect(s) of their roles. Such applies to all common terms such as Isis, Osiris, Amun, Re, Horus, etc.

4. When using the Latin calendar, we will use the following terms:

> **BCE** – Before Common Era. Also noted in other references as BC.
>
> **CE** – Common Era. Also noted in other references as AD.

5. There were/are no Ancient Egyptian writings/texts that were categorized by the Egyptians themselves as "religious", "funerary", "sacred", etc. Western academia gave the Ancient Egyptian texts arbitrary names, such as the "Book of This" and the "Book of That", "divisions", "utterances", "spells", etc. Western academia even decided that a certain "Book" had a "Theban version" or "this or that time period version". After believing their own inventive creation, academia then accused the Ancient Egyptians of making mistakes and missing portions of their own writings (?!!).

For ease of reference, we will mention the common but arbitrary Western academic categorization of Ancient Egyptian texts, even though the Ancient Egyptians themselves never did.

MAP OF ANCIENT EGYPT

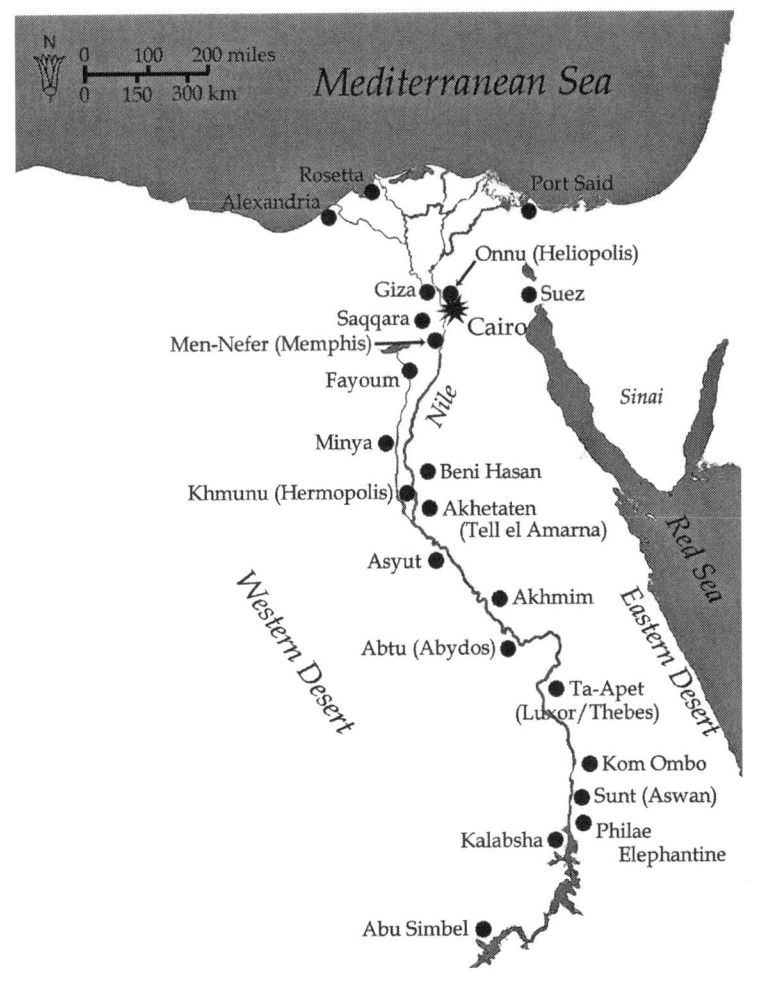

CHAPTER 1 : HISTORICAL DECEPTION OF THE (ANCIENT) EGYPTIAN LINGUISTICS

1.1 THE IMAGERY AND ALPHABETICAL WRITING MODES

All early Greek and Roman writers affirmed that there were basically two forms of Ancient Egyptian writings: hieroglyphs (pictorial images) and the alphabetical form. Western academia arbitrarily splits the Ancient Egyptian alphabetical type into two forms—hieratic and demotic. [Read about the evaluation of such unfounded assertions in *The Ancient Egyptian Universal Writing Modes* by Moustafa Gadalla.]

It must be emphasized that not a single classical writer—including Clement of Alexandria (in *Stromata Book V,* Chapter IV) — ever indicated that the Egyptian alphabetical form of writing was a "cursive" or "degenerated" form of the Ancient Egyptian pictorial hieroglyphics. Yet, shamelessly, some "scholars" invoked the writing of Clement of Alexandria to insist that out of Egyptian hieroglyphs sprang a more cursive writing known to us as *hieratic*, and out of *hieratic* there again emerged a very rapid script sometimes called *enchorial* or *demotic*.

Many honest scholars, however, confirmed the historical truth that the pictorial writings are a series of images conveying conceptual meanings and not individual sound values, such as the British Egyptologist W.M. Flinders Petrie, who wrote in his book, *The Formation of the Alphabets* [pg. 6]:

> *"The question as to whether the [alphabetical] signs were derived from the more pictorial hieroglyphs, or were an independent system, has been so little observed by writers on the subject, that the matter has been decided more than once without any consideration of the various details involved."*

In the 12th Dynasty (2000-1780 BCE), about 700 signs were in more or less constantly used. There are practically unlimited numbers of these natural symbols. Since deciphering the metaphysical Ancient Egyptian hieroglyphs is beyond Western academia's capabilities, they have dubbed it a *primitive* form of writing!

Academic Egyptologists cavalierly chose 24 signs out of hundreds of hieroglyphs, and called them an 'alphabet'. Then they gave various "functions" to the other hundreds of signs, calling them "syllabic", "determinative", etc. They made up the rules as they went along, and the end result was chaos. One can easily see the struggle of academia to understand the Ancient Egyptian hieroglyphic (metaphysical) texts.

A pictorial sign has NO SINGULAR sound value. Only an individual alphabetical letter has a corresponding singular sound—which was the case in the TOTALLY unrelated alphabetical language of the Ancient Egyptians known as "hieratic" and "demotic" writings—a very distinct and independent form that has nothing to do with the Egyptian hieroglyphic form of cosmic communications. Read more about the alphabetical language of the Ancient Egyptians in *The Ancient Egyptian Universal Writing Modes* by Moustafa Gadalla.

The Egyptian hieroglyph metaphysical language is consistent with the fact that there are, indeed, things that cannot be put into words. They make themselves manifest. They are what is mystical. Confronted by these mystical 'things', the reality which authorizes speech and words are condemned to deal only with appearances. Reality—whether logical form or forms of life— remains obstinately outside speech. It constrains what we say, yet refuses to be spoken. Unless we concede the existence of a transcendent reality outside speech, we become solipsists with no grounds for speaking. So, speaking depends upon silence. We can only speak together by consigning the grounds of our speaking to a respectful silence.

1.2 THE UNIVERSAL PICTORIAL SIGNS

Signs are everywhere around us. Arrows tell us where to go or where to look. Commas and periods show us when to pause as we read. In mathematics, signs tell us to add or subtract or divide. Traffic signs help drivers to drive carefully and pedestrians to cross the street safely.

None of the above signs depend on words. All of them can be understood by people who speak different languages—if they have learned what the signs mean.

In fact, every branch of scientific knowledge has its own

signs for communicating its own special kind of information. It would be impossible for everyone to understand all the signs in all the sciences. Nor do we need to.

A symbol, by definition, is not what it represents, but what it stands for; what it suggests. A symbol reveals to the mind a reality other than itself. Words convey information; symbols evoke understanding.

Symbols are the unspoken language, and the Egyptian hieroglyphs are likewise do not represent letters or words, but ideas and concepts.

1.3 THE EGYPTIAN PICTORIAL METAPHYSICAL IMAGES/SCRIPT

The Ancient Egyptians' pictorial system is commonly called 'hieroglyphs', which comprises a large number of pictorial symbols. The word hieroglyph means 'holy script' (*hieros* = holy, *glyphein* = impress). Hieroglyphic writing was in use in Egyptian temples until about 400 CE.

Each pictorial image is worth a thousand words and represents that function or principle on all levels simultaneously, from the simplest, most obvious physical manifestation of that function to the most abstract and metaphysical. This symbolic language represents a wealth of physical, physiological, psychological and spiritual ideas in the presented symbols.

The metaphorical and symbolic concept of the Egyptian hieroglyphs was unanimously acknowledged by all early writers on the subject, such as Plutarch, Diodorus, Clement, etc.

- In his treatise on Isis and Osiris, which is one of the most instructive sources for our understanding of Egyptian religious ideas, Plutarch mentions the hieroglyphs and their metaphorical and allegorical significance, in several places. In his *Moralia, Vol. V*, Plutarch states:

    "The <u>babe</u> is the symbol of coming into the world and the <u>aged man</u> the symbol of departing from it, and by a <u>hawk</u> they indicate God, by the <u>fish</u> hatred, and by the <u>hippopotamus</u> shamelessness."

    Plutarch, like ALL classical writers of his era, emphasized metaphysical intent as the sole principle of hieroglyphic writing, which is a pictorial expression of divine ideas and sacred knowledge.

    Plutarch listed an extensive number of distinguished Greeks who visited Egypt at different times. Among them, he mentioned Pythagoras, whose admiration and dependence on 'the symbolic and occult teachings of the Egyptians' is emphasized and illustrated by a comparison of the allegorical method used in the so-called Pythagorean precepts and *'the writings that are called hieroglyphs'*.

- Chairemon lived in Alexandria before he went to Rome, where he was the tutor of Nero from 49 CE onward. Chairemon described 19 hieroglyphic signs in his books, followed by an explanation of the allegorical significance of each.

- Diodorus of Sicily, in his *Book I*, stated:

    "Their—the Egyptians'—writing does not express the

intended concept by means of syllables joined one to another, but by means of the significance of the objects that have been copied, and by its figurative meaning that has been impressed upon the memory by practice. For instance they draw the picture of a hawk, a crocodile ... and the like. Now <u>the hawk signifies to them everything which happens swiftly, since this animal is practically the swiftest of winged creatures</u>. And the concept portrayed is then transferred, by the appropriate metaphorical transfer, to all swift things and to everything to which <u>swiftness</u> is appropriate, very much as if they had been named. And the <u>crocodile is a symbol of all that is evil</u>."

- Clement of Alexandria, in about 200 CE, gave an account of the hieroglyphs. The metaphorical and allegorical qualities of the hieroglyphs are at the same time explicitly mentioned, and his examples are expounded in the same symbolic way as those of earlier writers.

- The best description came from Plotinus, who wrote in *The Enneads* [Vol. V-VI]:

<u>"The wise men of Egypt, either by scientific or innate knowledge</u>, and when they wished to signify something wisely, did not use the forms of letters which follow the order of words and propositions and imitate sounds and the enunciations of philosophical statements, but by drawing images and inscribing in their temples one particular image of each particular thing, they manifested the non-discursiveness of the intelligible world, that is, that every image is a kind of knowledge and wisdom and is a subject of statements, all together in

one, and not discourse or deliberation. But [only] afterwards [others] discovered, starting from it in its concentrated unity, a representation in something else, already unfolded and speaking it discursively and giving the reasons why things are like this, so that, because what has come into existence is so beautifully disposed, if anyone knows how to admire it he expresses his admiration of how this wisdom, which does not itself possess the reasons why substance is as it is, gives them to the things which are made according to it."

Egyptian hieroglyphics may appear to be an unnecessary burden that the Egyptian priests have "invented" to maintain secrets away from other people. The fact of the matter is that such perceptions are far from the truth, on all accounts. Explanations will unfold to show that the concept of pictorial images in the Egyptian Hieroglyphics is the common denominator between all human beings everywhere and the divine forces of the universe.

CHAPTER 2 : THE SCIENTIFIC/METAPHYSICAL REALITIES OF PICTORIAL IMAGES

2.1 IMAGES: LANGUAGE OF THE MIND/CONSCIOUSNESS/DIVINE

As human beings, we say to each other:

- **PICTURE** this.
- Can you **IMAGINE** ….?
- Do you **SEE** my point?

The use of such words as PICTURE—IMAGINE—SEE my point—are deep reflections of how our minds process information that reaches us through our senses. We process ALL incoming information through IMAGES.

Linguistic communication consists of the transmission of immaterial ideas or concepts from one person (speaker or writer) to another (hearer or listener) by means of material signs such as marks on paper or vibrations of the air waves.

In reading a text, we undertake a process of vision whereby material signs are translated into concepts in our brains.

The traditional interpretation of communication purports to treat the material sign as the mere appearance of an underlying ideal reality.

When communication is interpreted in this way, the interplay of signs is not treated as a reality in its own right. Rather, the sign is taken as the signifier, indicator, or appearance of a signified essential reality which underlies it. This reality is the conceptual content which is somehow held in the brain of the communicating person.

This apparent modern thinking was known not only to the Ancient Egyptians, as we check the text of the *Shabaka Stele* that dates only to 700 BCE, but linguistic, philological, and other evidence is conclusive in support of its derivation from an original text at least more than 2,000 years earlier. Section 55 of this Egyptian document reads:

> *"The sight of the eyes, the hearing of the ears, and the smelling the air by the nose, they report to the heart. It is this which causes every completed (concept) to come forth, and it is the tongue that announces what the heart thinks. The senses report to the heart, With this report material, the heart conceives and releases thought, which the tongue, as a herald, puts into effective utterance."*

The *heart* in Ancient Egypt symbolizes the consciousness. As such, the information channeled via the five powers of sensation are brought to the faculty of the imagination whose physical dwelling place is the frontal lobe of the brain.

The data gathered by the five senses—this intimate,

received knowledge—is unified by the imagination. The imaginative 'welding' process does not follow the path of reason and logic. The mind amasses perceptual data and makes "sense" out of them. In turn, the imagination unifies in a similar, non-logical, manner.

The imagination moves from one thing to another. Given many things of nearly totally divergent natures but possessing one-thousandth part of a quality in common (provided that it be new or distinguished), these things belong in an imaginative category and not in a gross natural array – that is, not in a collection of data arrived at by mere copying. Language opened the new realm of spirituality where concepts, memories, and deductions became of decisive importance in contrast to lower psychical activity, which concerned itself with the immediate perceptions of the sense organs. It was certainly one of the most important stages on the way to becoming human.

As such, representative true images in the mind/consciousness are the true realities of the universe. It should be concluded then that a full correspondence between consciousnesses and world exists. It is the transcendentalist consciousness which gives rise to the mundane heaven, again with the necessary additional feature to preserve it as heaven, that its occupants know that they are there. More precisely, they are certain of the correspondence between consciousness and consciousness, and so goes any possible consciousness; and so, the world.

2.2 THE SOUNDNESS OF THE THREE ROLES OF EACH EGYPTIAN HIEROGLYPHIC IMAGE

The 'Hieroglyphics' of Horapollo is the only true hieroglyphic treatise preserved from classical antiquity. It consists of two books, one containing 70 chapters and the other 119; each dealing with one particular hieroglyph.

The relationships between sign and meaning were, according to Horapollo, always of an allegorical nature, and it was always established by means of 'philosophical' reasoning.

Accordingly, each Egyptian hieroglyph has a short heading describing either the hieroglyph itself in simple terms (as, for instance, 'the explanation of the picture of a falcon'), or else stating the nature of the allegorical subject to be explained, such as 'how to signify eternity' or 'how to signify the universe'.

Likewise, Clement of Alexandria, in *Stromata Book V*, chapter IV, tells us the two main roles (Literal and Symbolic) of the Egyptian hieroglyphs, and how the later (**Symbolic**) contains two roles—being **figurative** and **allegoric [mystical]**:

> *"The Egyptian Hieroglyphic, of which one aspect is by the first elements is literal, and the other Symbolic.*
>
> *Of the Symbolic, one kind speaks literally by imitation, and another writes as it were figuratively; and another is quite allegorical, using certain enigmas."*

[I] On the first role/subject—literally, by imitation—Clement's *Stromata Book V*, chapter IV, continues:

> *"Wishing to express Sun in writing, they make a circle; and Moon, a figure like the Moon, like its proper shape".*

[II] On the second role/subject—**figurative**—Clement's *Stromata Book V,* Chapter IV, continues:

> "But in using the figurative style, by transposing and transferring,
> by changing and by transforming in many ways as suits them, they draw characters".

[III] On the third role/subject—**allegorical**—Clement's *Stromata Book V,* Chapter IV, continues:

> "Let the following stand as a specimen of the third species-the Enigmatic. For the rest of the stars, on account of their oblique course, they have figured like the bodies of serpents; but the sun, like that of a beetle, because it makes a round figure of ox-dung, and rolls it before its face. And they say that this creature lives six months under ground, and the other division of the year above ground, and emits its seed into the ball, and brings forth; and that there is not a female beetle."

Clement, like ALL classical writers of antiquities, asserted that the Egyptian hieroglyphics represent true images of the divine law. The relationships between sign and meaning were always of an allegorical nature, and it was always established by means of 'philosophical' reasoning.

To summarize, the symbolic hieroglyphic writing is basically divided into three roles:

1) the Imitative (an object represents itself)
2) the Figurative (an object stands for one of its qualities); and

3) the Allegorical (an object is linked through enigmatic conceptual processes)

In fact, these categories describe relationships between visual forms and their meanings. A visual form may be mimetic or imitative, directly copying features of the object it represents; it may be associative, suggesting attributes which are not visually present such as abstract properties incapable of literal depiction; and finally, it may be symbolic, meaningful only when decoded according to conventions or systems of knowledge which, though not inherently visual, are communicated through visual means.

Each particular hieroglyph can be expounded from

- obvious/direct meaning of the sign, or
- by each's specific employments in the various contexts.

The rules governing the conception of allegories and symbols, with their subtle distinctions between cyriologic, tropological metaphorical, anaglyphical, and enigmatical comparisons, made such symbolic interpretations possible.

Such hieroglyphic expoundings combine the total religious, philosophic, and scientific knowledge into a grand vision of a living cosmology.

All ancient writers of antiquity agree, such as the neo-Platonist philosopher Lamblichus, who wrote, in his *De Mysteries*: *"The Egyptian hieroglyphic characters were not fortuitously or foolishly made, but with great ingenuity, after the example of Nature. Various Hebrew and Arabic authors concurred. They enshrine 'not histories or eulogies of kings, but the highest mysteries of Divinity."*

The triple-layered aspects of Egyptian hieroglyphic images are consistent with the general Egyptian thinking of the transcendentalist consciousness—the correspondence between consciousness and consciousness—and so goes any possible consciousness; and so, the world. In the Egyptian texts, there is no artificial distinction between 'sacred' and 'mundane.'

This is the basis of the 'theory of correspondences', and indeed of all traditional symbolism in which a true symbol is imbued with some of the power of its original. Contrary to the anthropological view of the origin of symbols in mere similarities, this doctrine regards them as primary realities whose actual relationship is perceived by man's higher intellect.

There must be something identical in a picture and what it depicts—an identity of the 'latent structure.'

The ideogram is an accurate mode of depicting reality. The traditional interpretation of communication purports to treat the material sign as the mere appearance of an underlying ideal reality.

Depiction is not synonymous with copying nature; ideogrammic writing is mimetic only in the sense that it attempts to enact natural processes.

The difference between pictures and world is that the

world is 'the sum-total of reality', but a picture only 'represents a situation in logical space'.

Ideograms may be defined to be pictures intended to represent either things or thoughts. There are two kinds of ideograms:

> 1) Pictures or actual representations of objects;
> 2) Pictorial symbols, which are used to suggest abstract ideas.

2.3 THE INTERPRETATION PROCESS OF SERIAL IMAGES IN THE CONSCIOUSNESS

1. Interpretation of Ideogrammic Streams

Clement of Alexandria, in his *Stromata, Book V,* chapter VII, gives a sample of what a series of Egyptian Hieroglyphic images/ideograms convey:

> *"Further, at Diospolis in Egypt, on the temple called Pylon, there was figured a boy as the symbol of production, and an old man as that of decay. A hawk, on the other hand, was the symbol of God, as a fish of hate; and, according to a different symbolism, the crocodile; of impudence. The whole symbol, then, when put together, appears to teach this: "Oh ye who are born and die, God hates impudence."*

I.J. Gelb, in his book *A Study of Writing: The Foundation of Grammatology,* page 36, expressed this pictorial form of writing:

> *"Expressing ideas discussed here give attention to the*

purposes for which they are used and to the way in which they are achieved.

The examples quoted above all serve to communicate men's ideas by means of pictures, each of which separately, or their sum total, suggests the intended meaning. For this reason this stage of writing has sometimes been called <u>'thought writing', 'representational writing', or 'content writing'.</u>

The picture or a series of pictures describe to the eye what the eye sees in a way parallel to that achieved by the picture originated under the artistic-aesthetic urge. To be sure, there are differences between the schematic execution of pictures intended to convey one's ideas and that of pictures made for artistic reasons, but the general similarities between the two entirely overshadow the existent divergences. This stage of the forerunners of writing could therefore be called the 'descriptive' or 'representational' stage, using a term which points toward a close connection in the technique of expression in writing and in art."

Laszlo Gefin, in his book *Ideogram: History of Poetic Method*, pages 16-17, concurs with the Egyptian intent of images/ideograms form of writing:

"The flow of thought follows a natural pattern instead of merely an arbitrary one. Thought is successive, because the operations of nature are successive. The transferences of force from agent to object, which constitute natural phenomena, occupy time.

This group of symbols is "alive," it is something like "a

continuous moving picture."
<u>Pictures do not depict things but actions and processes.</u>

<u>Two things added together do not produce a third thing but suggest some fundamental relation between them.</u> Giving us "vivid shorthand pictures of actions and processes in nature.

These symbols do not only represent natural images but lofty thoughts, spiritual suggestions and obscure relations. The idea of <u>"latent structure"</u> behind the scheme of things is formulated thus: "The greater part of natural truth is hidden in processes too minute for vision and in harmonies too large, in vibrations, cohesions, and in affinities.

The larger and more important part of natural truth is hidden from the physical eye, yet it is no less real. It is hidden both in the processes too minute for vision, and in harmonies too large; in vibrations, cohesions, affinities; in orders, analogies, proportions, affections and character. <u>Virtue, religion, beauty, law, social amenities, family ties, political responsibilities, all these exhibit immaterial planes of true being</u>, in which the chief poetic values of the world are realized."

Ideogrammic streams provide an underlining of the "cinematic visuality" and the paratactic formation of lines in Egyptian depictions so that the natural actuality of "things in motion, motion in things" is not lost. The successive Egyptian hieroglyphic images do not constitute a linear development (such as how this leads to that). Rather, the objects coexist, as in a painting, and yet the mobile point of view has made it possible to temporalize the spatial units. Immaterial relations are depicted by juxtaposing pertinent concrete data in a suggestive way. This simultaneity of perceptual units and their actions in a functional whole is the essence of Egyptian ideograms.

2. Interpretation of the Ideogrammic Streams of Dreams

As stated earlier, the faculties through which the body perceives knowledge are all connected with the brain. The active part among them is the imagination. It derives imaginary pictures from the pictures perceived by the senses and turns them over to the power of memory, which retains them until they are needed in connection with speculation and deduction.

From the imaginary pictures, the soul also abstracts other spiritual-intellectual pictures. In this way, abstraction ascends from the sensibilia to the intelligibilia. The imagination is the intermediary between them. Also, when the soul has received a certain number of perceptions from its own world, it passes them on to the imagination, which forms them into appropriate pictures and turns those perceptions over to common sense. As a result, the sleeper sees them as if they were perceived by the senses. Thus, the perceptions come down from the rational spirit to the level of sensual perception, with the imagination again being the intermediary. This is what dream visions actually are. Consciousness itself is a dream.

The preceding exposition shows the difference between true dream visions and false, 'confused dreams'. All of them are pictures in the imagination while an individual is asleep. However, if these pictures come down from the rational spirit that perceives them, they are dream visions. But if they are derived from the pictures preserved in the power of memory, where the imagination deposits them when the individual is awake, they are 'confused dreams'.

As for dream interpretation, the following should be known. The rational spirit has its perceptions and passes them on to the imagination. The imagination then forms them into pictures, but it forms them only into such pictures as are somehow related to the perceived idea. For instance, if the idea of a mighty ruler is perceived, the imagination depicts it in the form of an ocean. Or, the idea of hostility is depicted by the imagination in the form of a serpent. A person wakes up and knows only that he saw an ocean or a serpent. Then the dream interpreter, who is certain that the ocean is the picture conveyed by the senses and that the perceived idea is something beyond that picture, puts the power of comparison to work. He is guided by further data that establish the character of the perceived idea for him.

When the spirit passes its perceptions to the imagination, the latter depicts them in the customary molds of sensual perception. Where such molds never existed in sensual perception, the imagination cannot form any pictures. A person who was born blind could not depict a ruler by an ocean, an enemy by a serpent, or women by vessels, because he had never perceived any such things. For him, the imagination would depict those things through similarly appropriate pictures derived from the type of perceptions with which he is familiar—that is, things which can be heard or smelled. The dream interpreter must be on guard against such things. They often cause confusion in dream interpretation and spoil its rules.

3. Analogy as the Agent of Imagination [Figurative-Allegorical]

Analogy is the relationship established by the imagination between two or several essentially different objects of thought. Analogy is, then, the work of mind. It expresses an 'imagination' which establishes a relation between 'objects of thought'. Analogy offers an imaginary relationship. A relationship established by the imagination is nonetheless postulated as expressing a natural order.

The reductivist impulse reigns supreme in the work of analogy. Signs are inevitably seen as signs of something else; activities are treated as documents of an underlying reality. So interpretation is the aim of all understanding, and interpretation is achieved when the pattern supposedly submerged in the appearance is noticed and named (analogy, metaphor, etc.).

The turn towards analogy expresses the practice of 'interpretation'. It is a practice which seems eminently 'realistic' in demanding a signified for every signifier, and in insisting that signs must be 'of' something.

But this 'realism' is the grossest idealism. Nature itself is a work of signs. The signs speak Nature.

Ancient Egyptians believe in the truth of allegory, and not the allegory itself: the coalescence of the sign, the similitude of signifier and signified, the homeomorphism of images, the Mirror, or the captivating 'bait'.

In analogy, the signifier coalesces with the signified: it seems to stand in for, or to mark, Nature. So, signs are the 'Mirror' of Nature. Their internal relationships (analogy, metaphor) appear as natural and insistent prepositions ('of', 'about') that establish them as frames of Nature. To resist analogy is to resist this (imaginary) Nature – to reclaim the natural for the textual.

CHAPTER 3 : EGYPTIAN HIEROGLYPHIC IMAGERY DEPICTION OF THOUGHTS

3.1 IDEOGRAMS OF IDEAS [IMAGES AS METAPHYSICAL SYMBOLS]

It is worth repeating Plotinus' description of how the Egyptians came up with their pictographic hieroglyphic ideograms. Plotinus wrote. in *The Enneads* [Vol. V-VI]:

> "*The wise men of Egypt, either by scientific or innate knowledge,* and when they wished to signify something wisely, did not use the forms of letters which follow the order of words and propositions and imitate sounds and the enunciations of philosophical statements, but by drawing images and inscribing in their temples one particular image of each particular thing, they manifested the non-discursiveness of the intelligible world, that is, that *every image is a kind of knowledge and wisdom and is a subject of statements, all together in one*, and not discourse or deliberation. But [only] afterwards [others] discovered, *starting from it in its concentrated unity, a representation in something else, already unfolded* and speaking it discursively and giving the reasons why things are like this, so that, because what has come into existence is so beautifully

disposed, if anyone knows how to admire it he expresses his admiration of how this wisdom, which does not itself possess the reasons why substance is as it is, <u>gives them to the things which are made according to it</u>."

In this Egyptian meta-language, both the Signifier and Signified of the Sign dissolve by use of the sign that ultimately represents extra-linguistic 'signified' concepts or a signified reality.

The linguistic sign unites not a thing and a name, but a concept. The link would be between, on the one hand, a psychological entity (in the case of a concept) and, on the other hand, a material entity. The contrast is at once between the subjective and the objective, the ideal and the material, and the private and the social.

Egyptians never differentiated between "sacred" and "mundane" (two sides of the same coin) images of each other, always aware of maintaining this relationship between Above and Below and vice versa.

Egyptian hieroglyphic ideograms are formed in accordance with natural laws. The character of the Egyptian written sign inheres in this natural capacity to recreate processes.

Ideograms may be defined as pictures intended to represent either things or thoughts. There are two kinds of Ideograms:

1. Pictures, or actual representations of objects.
To copy is merely to reflect something already there,

inert. Through imitation, we enlarge nature itself and become nature; or we discover in ourselves nature's active part.

2. Pictorial symbols, which are used to suggest abstract ideas.

Imitation through imagination means creating art objects to be set beside the natural objects of the world. The method of artistic creation and the shape of the object created are specifically human realizations of the universal creative forces present in nature. It is the force of the imagination through which we can feel ourselves related, sympathetically, to the larger "latent" force of the cosmos. In creating new objects with the aid of the imagination, the mystic does not desert reality by constructing things alien and unnatural. Imagination does not tamper with the world, but moves it in accordance with nature.

3.2 AN OVERVIEW OF THE EGYPTIAN FORMATION OF IDEOGRAMS

1. The Wealth of Knowledge in the Egyptian Pictorial Formations

A symbol, by definition, is not what it represents, but what it stands for; what it suggests. A symbol reveals to the mind a reality other than itself. Words convey information; symbols evoke understanding.

A chosen symbol represents that function or principle on all levels simultaneously—from the simplest, most obvious physical manifestation of that function to the most abstract and metaphysical. Without recognizing the simple fact about the intent of symbolism, we will continue to be ignorant of the wealth of Egyptian knowledge and wisdom.

This symbolic language represents a wealth of physical, physiological, psychological, and spiritual data in the symbols/signs.

2. Man depiction signifies The Universe

Many phrases are being used throughout the world which consistently state that the human being is made in the image of God – i.e., a miniature universe – and that to understand the universe is to understand oneself, and vice versa.

Yet, no culture has ever practiced these principle like the Ancient Egyptians. Central to their complete understanding of the universe was the knowledge that man was made in the image of God and, as such, man represented the image of all creation.

Consistent with such thinking, a depicted human being represents both the universe as a whole as well as the human being, on Earth. The difference between the two will be clear in the context of the text.

3. Animal Symbolism

Egyptians' careful observation and profound knowledge of the natural world enabled them to identify certain animals with specific qualities that could symbolize certain divine functions and principles in a particularly pure and striking fashion.

When we talk about loyalty, there is no better way to express loyalty than by a dog.

When we talk about the protective aspect of motherhood, there is no better way to express it than with a lioness.

This symbolic expression of deep-spiritual understanding was presented in three main forms. The first and second are animal-headed humans, or a pure animal form.

The third form is the opposite of the animal-headed human. In this case, we have a human-headed bird—such as the Ba—representing the body soul hovering over the body. The depiction of the Ba, then, is the divine aspect of the terrestrial.

4. Accessories, Emblems, Color, etc.

In Egyptian symbolism, the precise role of the *neteru* (gods/goddesses) are revealed in many ways: by dress, headdress, crown, feather, animal, plant, color, position, size, gesture, sacred object (flail, scepter, staff, ankh), etc. This symbolic language represents a wealth of physical, physiological, psychological, and spiritual data in the presented symbols.

5. Action Forms

Practically all figures on the walls of Egyptian monuments are in profile form, indicative of action and interaction between the various symbolic figures. A wide variety of actions in the forms are evident.

One must view these depictions in the proper perspective (how does this series of depictions relate to each other?), but first, how do these depictions fit in the overall picture (in the context of the text)?

6. Orientations of Hieroglyphic Characters

Hieroglyphic characters may be written in columns or in horizontal lines, which are sometimes to be read from left to right and sometimes from right to left. There was no fixed rule about the direction in which the characters should be written, but the heads always turned towards the beginning of the sentence.

The orientation of the characters could be affected by a multitude of factors, such as the type of material written on, the position of the text in relation to figures or other texts, or the nature of the inscription. In certain cases, texts were deliberately written backwards. There are also examples of inscriptions that make sense only when read from bottom to top!

Hieroglyphic characters are arranged in a stream of hieroglyphic text in:

>   **a**. Singular forms
>   **b**. A single symbol in double or triple form to reflect duality or plurality.
>   **c**. A combined two symbols in one form such as a leg with a knife to indicate a combined meaning of 'no trespassing.'
>   **d**. A cluster/group of separated 2-3 images showing a loose connectivity of specific thought/concept in a dual or triple structure.

In the following chapters more detailed information will

be provided about a large sample of Egyptian hieroglyphics, divided into five groups—Chapters 4 through 8:

    4. Animal Hieroglyphic Images
    5. Human and Animal-headed Human Hieroglyphic Images
    6. Human Body Parts Hieroglyphic Images
    7. Nature and Geometrical Figure Hieroglyphic Images
    8. Manmade Object Hieroglyphic Images

CHAPTER 4 : ANIMAL HIEROGLYPHIC IMAGES

4.1 METAPHYSICAL SIGNIFICANCE OF ANIMAL IMAGES

The primary function of the Egyptian Ideograms is to represent thoughts. This means that one must be searching for both the Figurative (an object stands for one of its qualities) and the Allegorical (an object is linked through enigmatic conceptual processes).

We must always keep in mind the relationships between visual forms and their meanings. A visual form may be mimetic or imitative, directly copying features of the object it represents; it may be associative, suggesting attributes which are not visually present such as abstract properties incapable of literal depiction; and finally, it may be symbolic, meaningful only when decoded according to conventions or systems of knowledge which, though not inherently visual, are communicated through visual means.

As noted earlier, the Egyptians' careful observation and profound knowledge of the natural world enabled them to identify certain animals with specific qualities that could symbolize certain divine functions and principles in a particularly pure and striking fashion. As such, certain animals were chosen as symbols for that particular aspect of divinity. The more we learn about these animals' behaviors, etc., the more we realize/recognize their possible meanings.

Animals and their body parts are also referred to, by the Ancient Egyptians, in defining the perimeters of the astronomical constellations, such as:

> Bull Leg (Great Bear)
> Claw of the Goose
> Head of the Goose
> Hinderpart of the Goose
> Head of the Lion
> Tail of the Lion

The star chart of the north pole of the sky from the tomb of Seti I [1333–1304 BCE] reinforces the Ancient Egyptian meaning of the word 'zodiac' as a circle of animals [read *Ancient Egyptian Culture Revealed* by Moustafa Gadalla, for detailed information.]

4.2 SAMPLE RELATED EGYPTIAN HIEROGLYPHIC IMAGES

Animal-related Egyptian hieroglyphic images are found in sections E, F, G, H, I, Y, K & L of the standard *List of Hieroglyphics* [available on the internet].

Next is a section of selected Egyptian hieroglyphic images with animal related pictographs, with a very brief review of each's metaphysical functions/attributes, to help stay away from silly Western academics' descriptions and in order to focus on their REAL subtle/deep meanings. It is always helpful to think of 'figures of speech' related to each image, in order to recognize each one's nature/behavior/characteristics/attributes.

Ass [E 7]

The ass represents the Ego and stubbornness as an aspect of the neter (god) Seth.

The ass may also represents hard work.

It may also represent fertility, where the male has a very strong phallus erection.

Ba [G 53]

The Ba is one of the metaphysical components of the human (and other) beings.

The Ba is immortal. When the Ba departs, the body dies. The Ba is represented as a human-headed bird, which is the opposite of the normal depiction of *neteru* (gods, goddesses) as human bodies with animal heads—in other words, as the divine aspect of the terrestrial. The Ba may be shown as a stork or as a falcon. The stork is known for its migrating and homing instinct. The stork is known worldwide as the bird that carries newborn babies to their new families. The stork returns to its own nest with consistent precision – hence a migratory bird, par excellence, is the bird chosen for the soul. 'Ba' is usually translated as 'soul'.

Baboon [E 32-33]

The baboon is almost human, and as such, it represents this crucial moment that precedes the awakening of the sun.

The baboon emits a crackling sound at the crack of dawn—The Point of Beginning. The baboon represents this point of beginning extremely well. The baboon represents the starting point of a Cycle—being a creation cycle or a daily cycle.

In such a role, the baboon is associated with Thoth [Tehuti], the divine intermediary between the metaphysical (the darkness before dusk) and the Physical (as in the daylight).

In Ancient Egyptian traditions, the words of Re, revealed through Thoth, became the things and creatures of this world, i.e. the words (meaning, sound energies) created the forms in the universe. As such, Thoth represents the link between the metaphysical (extra human) and the physical (terrestrial).

It is therefore that we find the baboon depicted as sitting and waiting for Moment Zero, or standing up and hailing the coming of a new cycle.

Consistent with the baboon's role, we find that one of the four Disciples of Horus is baboon-headed. His role is to watch over the Eastern quadrant, the region where new/renewed creation comes forth.

The baboon, like Thoth [Tehuti], is associated with the lunar principle.

Baby Chick [G 43-50]

It is obvious that a baby chick represents a new beginning.

Bee [L 2]

Various attributes are all related to the bee. The specific attribute will be determined by the context. Some related attributes are:

– Solar significance
– Symbol of the fecund bounty of the natural world
– Pollination
– Honey making and its benefits as food, medicine, etc.
– Work ethics (busy bee)
– Sting—as in bee sting

Beetle [L 1]

The scarab or dung beetle is one of the 75 Manifestations of the creation process, all being aspects of Re—the divine creative force.

Horapollo Niliaeus explains the symbolism of the scarab in this way:

> *"To signify the only begotten, or birth, or a father, or the world, or man, they [Egyptians] draw a scarab. The only begotten, because this animal is self-begotten, unborn of the female. For its birth takes place only in the following way. When the male wishes to have offspring, it takes some cow-*

dung and makes a round ball of it, very much in the shape of the world. Rolling it with its hind legs from east to west, it faces the east, so as to give it the shape of the world, for the world is borne from the east to the west."

The scarab beetle is therefore always found at the beginning of a cycle.

Re is frequently represented as a large black scarab beetle sitting in the solar boat and rolling the sun disc, or as a man whose human head is replaced by a scarab beetle.

As such, Re is the original divine scarab. The Egyptian name for the scarab beetle was Khepri, a multiple word meaning *'This who brings/comes into being'*.

Re is described in the *Unas Funerary (Pyramid) Texts*:

"They cause thee to come into being as Re, in the name of Khepri."

As such, the beetle relates to the solar principle.

Birds [G Ducks]

Bird catching depictions in Ancient Egyptian tombs and temples are the physical representation of metaphysical concepts.

Bird catching symbolizes the divine man taming the wild aspects of nature—being within our beings, or outside it.

For the Ancient Egyptians, each bird (such as the falcon, vulture, stork, phoenix, goose, etc.) symbolized various spiritual qualities. Each species of bird represented a wild spiritual aspect that must be trapped, caged, sometimes tamed, and other times offered to the *neteru* (gods, goddesses) in sacrifice.

Several kinds of birds are shown in hieroglyphic images—examples include geese, ducks, teal, quail, partridge, long-legged birds like cranes, waterfowl, and other various species.

Bulls [E 1-3] [F 13-15] [F 23-24]

Various attributes are all related to the bull. The specific attribute will be determined by the context.

1. Fertility and Sexual Powers [E 1—striding bull].The wild bull, which is a nearly universal symbol for sexual power, symbolizes boundless strength and fertility. Bulls are esteemed for their sexuality, for a single animal can impregnate an entire herd. As such, the wild bull is a symbol for untamed sexual energy.

The universe cannot exist without the ability to replicate, i.e. reproduce.

Clement of Alexandria wrote in his *Stromata Book V*, chapter VII:

> *"The bull [for the Egyptians] clearly is of the earth itself, and husbandry and food."*

The bulls were/are also associated with fertility rites, as explained by Diodorus in *Book I*, [21, 8-22]:

> *"The consecration to Osiris, however, of the sacred bulls, which are given the name of Apis and Mnevis, and the worship of them as gods were observed generally among all the Egyptians, since these animals had, more than any others, rendered aid to those who discovered the fruit of the grain, in connection with both the sowing of the seed and with every agricultural labor from which mankind profits.*

2. Symbolize wild aspects to be tamed [E 2—aggressive bull]. The bull represents this powerful sexual energy that must be tamed and managed.

Hunting wild animals represents the ability of us humans to control the wild aspects of nature, whether within our beings or outside it.

The divine man is shown dispersing and hunting all kinds of wild animals—including the wild bull.

3. Symbolize strength, determination, hard work [F 13-15—ox horns]. As noted by Horapollo, for the Egyptians, bull's horns depict work. This is similar to the saying in English-speaking countries: *"Take the bull by the Horn"* as a figure of speech to mean to 'take control and get the work done'.

4. Symbolize sacrifice—takes a life to save a life—renewal [E 2-3—calf]. Osiris represents the process, growth, and the underlying cyclical aspects of the universe—the principle that makes life come from apparent death.

The Egyptian word for a young bull is **A**. **G L** ;simply meaning a (male) cycle.

Osiris represents the rejuvenation/renewal principle in the universe. Therefore, in the Ancient Egypt context, the bull had to suffer a sacrificial death to ensure the life of the community. The sacrifice of the holy animal, and the eating of his flesh, brought about a state of grace.

Small tablets in Ancient Egyptian tombs sometimes represent a black bull bearing the corpse of a man to its final abode in the regions of the dead. The name of this bull is shown to be Apis because Osiris represents the state of death in everyone/thing—the divine in mortal form.

Throughout Egypt and in all eras, bulls are depicted in tombs and temples, to be sacrificed during the festivals to renew and to rejuvenate life.

It continues to be a common practice in present-day Egypt that young bulls are sacrificed upon a person's death. The same practice continues in thousands of annual folk saints' festivals in Egypt.

5. Astronomy—The bull is one of the zodiac signs [E 1—striding bull]

As a constellation the foreleg of the bull [F 23-24—leg of bull] It represents the constellation of Ursa major—The Big Dipper.

Cat [E 13]

In the *Litany of Re*, Re is described as **'The One of the Cat'**, and **'The Great Cat'**. The nine realms of the universe are manifested in the cat, for both the cat and the Grand Ennead (meaning, nine times—unity) have the same Ancient Egyptian term. This relationship has found its way into Western culture, where one says that the *cat has nine lives* (realms).

The cat represents the total harmony—the sense of internal happiness, contentment, and peace.

Cows [E 4-5 forms of cows] [E 4 Hesat]

Various attributes are all related to the cow and are depicted in various hieroglyphic images. The specific attribute will be determined by the context.

Cows generally represent nourishment, both physically and metaphysically—both on the celestial/cosmic level—as well as human level.

The cow is the ideal representation for nourishment of all kinds. The Ancient Egyptian texts describe Isis of the 10,000 names in her role of the cow-headed Hathor as:

> **The Cow Heru-sekha, who brings forth all things...**
>
> **Who nourished the child Horus with her milk.** [E 5]

We also have the hieroglyph for Hesat [E-4], a form of

Hathor whose function is to feed the youngsters.

Hesat represents the metaphysical nourishment (love, caring, singing, etc.) necessary for the growth and well-being of the children.

Hathor, as the symbol of spiritual nourishment, also plays an important role in the transformational (funerary) texts, furnishing the spiritual nourishment required by the soul of the deceased.

When the successful soul achieves reunification with the Source, he/she reaches the original Celestial Cow, where he/she will be enshrined for eternity.

Crododile [I 3-5]

Various attributes are all related to the crocodile. The specific attribute will be determined by the context, as being either 'good' or 'evil'.

1. Crocodile is an aspect manifestation of the solar principle. Reference is made here to Plutarch's *Moralia Volume V*:

> "*The crocodile, certainly, has acquired honor which is not devoid of a plausible reason, but he is declared to be a living representation of God, since he is the only creature without a tongue; for the Divine Word has no need of a voice.*"

2. The Egyptian word for crocodile is **Te- MSaHh**. Its verb form is **MaSaHh**, which means *to rub/anoint*.

The English word Messiah originated also from the

Hebrew and Aramic Mashih which, in its form as a verb, MeSHeH., means 'to anoint'. This word is of Egyptian origin, where MeSSeH [the letter *s* in Egyptian is equivalent to 'sh' in Hebrew and Aramaic] signified the ritual of anointing Ancient Egyptian Kings with the fat of crocodiles, as was the tradition with all kings in Ancient Egypt since at least 2700 BCE.

Anointing was a ritual of the coronation of the Egyptian King. Thus the Christ/Messiah means *the anointed one, who is the king.*

3. The concept of the birth of the Messiah without sexual intercourse originated in Ancient Egypt. Isis is said to have conceived her son Horus of this, after her husband Osiris' death.

The cosmic force responsible for her impregnation was **MeSSeH**, *the crocodile star*, as per Spell 148 of the *Coffin Texts*:

> **"The crocodile star (MeSSeH) strikes ... Isis wakes pregnant with the seed of Osiris—namely Horus".**

Horus is the result of the strike of the crocodile star.

4. The crocodile also has other significances/roles as it is portrayed in zodiac and astronomical scenes.

> – As one of the recognized constellations.
> – Always found in zodiac scenes standing at the beginning of the zodiac cycle, or in his normal horizontal position as an astronomical constellation.

5. The crocodile represents the end of the earthly voyage—death—that is necessary in order to achieve resurrection and eternal life. Without death, there can be no possibility of a return to the source.

Diodorus of Sicily wrote:

"The crocodile is significant of every kind of baseness."

Clement of Alexandria, in his *Stromata Book V,* chapter VII, wrote:

"The crocodile symbolizes impudence".

Dogs [E 14-19]

Various attributes are all related to the dog. There are several forms of dogs/jackal shown in various positions in various contexts. The specific attribute will be determined by the context.

1. The dog/jackal represents the right sense of direction—the Divine Guide.

The dog/jackal is famous for its reliable homing instinct, day or night. The dog is very useful in searches, and is the animal of choice to guide the blind. As such, it is an excellent choice for guiding the soul of the deceased through the regions of the Duat.

2. The metaphysical role of the dog is reflected in his diet. The dog/jackal feasts on carrion, turning it into beneficial nourishment. In other words, it represents the capacity to turn waste into useful food for the body (and soul).

3. The dog represents absolute loyalty.

4. The dog has other related manifestations to match its peculiar traits, such as presented in Clement's *Stromata, Book V,* Chapter VII:

> *"... For the dogs are symbols of the two hemispheres, which, as it were, go round and keep watch...*
>
> *And some will have it that by the dogs are meant the tropics, which guard and watch the sun's passage to the south and north.."*

5. The dog is also identified as being Sirius the Dog Star, which is related to:

> **a.** The star of Isis—The Great Provider
> **b.** The Point of Origin in the Egyptian Calendar
>
> **a.** Sirius—the Dog Star is identified as the dwelling place of the universal mother, Isis.
>
> During very remote periods of Ancient Egyptian history, Isis was associated with the star Sirius, the brightest star in heaven, which was called, like her, *the Great Provider* and whose annual rising ushered in the Nile's inundation.
>
> **b.** Egypt's ingenious and very accurate calendar was based on the observation and the study of Sirius' movements in the sky. This fact is clearly

acknowledged in the Webster's dictionary, which defines the Sothic year as:

> -of having to do with Sirius, the Dog Star
> -Designating or of an Ancient Egyptian cycle or period of time based on fixed year.

The Ancient Egyptians knew that the full year was slightly over 365¼ days. The earth takes 365.25636 days to complete one revolution around the sun—and that was/is the length of the Egyptian Sothic Year. [More details can be found in *Ancient Egyptian Culture Revealed* by Moustafa Gadalla.]

Egg [H 8]

Earlier, we talked about the significance of the (dung) beetle/scarab and how it forms and roll its fertile egg-shaped dung. This symbolizes the cosmic egg.

An egg represents the dwelling container where creation takes place—from a bird's egg to the egg-shaped universe.

The *Universal Bubble* is egg-shaped and therefore the universal womb/container/bubble is also called the Cosmic Egg.

Egyptian texts refer to Khnum as the one who:

"made the cosmic egg"

Khnum is also referred to as:

> *"Maker of heaven, and earth, and the Tuat, and water and the mountains".*

The Cosmic Egg has several inter-related meanings:

  a. the vehicle of the universal spirit
  b. the embodiment of power/vital force

Just as Khnum represents the divine shaping force of the whole universe, Khnum is also depicted fashioning the image of the miniature universe—man—on a potter's wheel.

Falcon [G 5—13]

Various attributes are all related to the falcon. There are several forms of the falcon, shown in various positions in various contexts. The specific attribute will be determined by the context.

1. Falcon(s) represent the universal solar principle, per Clement of Alexandria in his *Stromata, Book V*, Chapter VII:

> *"—the falcon symbolizes the sun, for it is fiery and destructive (so the Egyptians attribute pestilential diseases to the sun)..."*

2. The falcon is/was closely associated with Horus—a manifestation of the solar principle. In his *Moralia Vol. V*, Plutarch states,

> *"by a falcon they indicate god"*

In Clement of Alexandria's *Stromata Book V*, Chapter VII:

> "A falcon was the symbol of god"

3. Falcon(s) represent the equinoctial line, as per Clement of Alexandria in his *Stromata Book V*, Chapter VII:

> "The falcon signifies the equinoctial line, which is high and parched with heat...."

4. Falcon(s) represent swiftness, as per Diodorus of Sicily:

> *"The falcon signifies to them everything which happens swiftly, since this animal is practically the swiftest of winged creatures. And the concept portrayed is then transferred, by the appropriate metaphorical transfer, to all swift things and to everything to which swiftness is appropriate, very much as if they had been named".*

[Read *Egyptian Divinities* by Moustafa Gadalla for more details on Horus and falcons.]

Feather [H 6]

The tall ostrich plume/feather represents the weightlessness of the truth usually identified with Maat by a feather of truth mounted on her head.

Read more about its uses with Maat, other deities and its measure of pure consciousness in the typical Weighing of the Heart process at Judgment Day in *Egyptian Divinities* by Moustafa Gadalla.

Fish [K 1-7]

Various attributes are all related to the fish. The specific attribute will be determined by the context.

1. Fishing represents the ability to control the wild aspects of nature—either within our beings, or outside it.

Fishing scenes are plentiful in the Egyptian temples and tombs. In the Egyptian texts, Horus assumes the form of a fisherman, and his four disciples ("sons") also fish with him. Christ used similar symbolism by making his disciples 'fishers of men'.

2. Fish symbolize 'hate', as per Plutarch in his *Moralia Volume V*:

> *"by the fish* [Egyptians symbolized] **hatred***"*

A similar description by Clement of Alexandria in *Stromata Book V*, Chapter VII:

> *"fish symbolizes hate"*

This relates to the Osiris allegory when the Evil Seth and his accomplices cut Osiris body into pieces and his phallus was thrown into the Nile River where a fish ate it.

3. Fish stink like no other animal—therefore, a fish can also signify stinginess.

4. Fish also symbolize rebirth—abundance.

Frog [I 7]

Frogs represents conception and procreation, i.e. the source of life.

Male frogs are extremely prolific. Frogs are seen in vast numbers just before the annual flooding of the Nile, symbolizing new life.

Frogs are symbols of abundance, fertility, and resurrection/rebirth.

Frog amulets were/are popular in Egypt for fertility because of the frog's prolific nature.

Giraffe [E 27]

With their long necks giraffes are able to see/oversee/observe better than any land animal with their feet on the ground—with all the metaphysical considerations for such physical traits.

Goose [G 38-39]

The goose symbolizes/expresses the word 'son' in the Egyptian language because of that bird's intense love of its offspring, as confirmed by Horapollo.

It is also the goose that laid the golden egg—the source of creation.

Hare [E 34]

The hare's eyes always remain open. Such a physical feature symbolizes cosmic metaphysical concepts for the ever-open watchful divine eyes.

The long ears of this animal also signifies the divine hearing/listening.

Heron [Stork/Phoenix] [G 31-32]

The heron, stork and phoenix are intimately related. The phoenix was identified by the Egyptians as a stork or heron-like bird called a *benu/bennu*. Bennu is represented as a flying bird and is portrayed as a composite heron and stork, or as a composite of the falcon and stork. Some of its significant attributes are:

1. It represents rebirth, as the manifestation of the resurrected Osiris.

The stork is known for its migrating and homing instinct, and is also known worldwide as the bird that carries newborn babies to their new families.

Bennu, in the form of stork, brings a New Life.

The stork returns to its own nest with consistent precision—hence a migratory bird is the perfect choice to represent the soul returning to the Source.

Osiris represents the divine in a mortal form that lives, dies, and is reborn again. It is therefore that the soul of Osiris dwells in the bird Bennu—who is always found near scenes of resurrection.

Every deceased person is Osiris, and will be resurrected and reborn again.

2. It represents the state of gaining/regaining consciousness.

3. As symbol for rebirth, it is associated with the solar principle.

4. It is also referred to as symbol of planet Venus, with all that implies.

The heron is presented in two positions—inactive/perching or active/striding.

> **a.** At the Source, it is depicted as perched on Benben—the symbol of the primeval hill. In this regard, it is the Phoenix rising from the ashes of the primeval hill to start another life.
>
> **b.** Striding to lead all creations to the Source.

It is a continuous cycle of bringing forth and returning to the Source.

Bennu, as such, is a symbol of resurrection and there were formulae instructing the deceased on how to become the Benu.

Hippopotamus [E 25]

Various attributes are all related to the hippopotamus. The specific attribute will be determined in the context being either 'good' or 'evil'.

1. Being of destructive nature, it is considered One of Seth's animals. This is confirmed in Plutarch's *Moralia Volume V*:

"by the hippopotamus shamelessness"

2. The huge size of the hippopotamus projects its maternal/childbearing attributes, and is thus a symbol of fertility.

3. The mother animal is known for the fearless protection of their young.

4. As "mother of all", its upright form is found at the beginning of each cycle—such as the zodiac cycle—as depicted in numerous places throughout Egypt prior to the Greek era.

5. As the bearer/container of all creation, it is found in all rebirth scenes, cosmic and otherwise.

6. In astronomy, the hippopotamus is one of the northern circumpolar constellations.

Hoopoe [G 22]

In the Egyptian mystical poem "Conference of the Birds", the hoopoe is chief of the troop of birds who set out looking for the Simurg or divine principle. In this Sufi allegory, the hoopoe is feminine.

Of special interest is the consistent showing of an Ancient Egyptian adult with his son, wearing the sidelock of youth and carrying the hoopoe.

Horse [E 6]

Various attributes are all related to the horse. The specific attribute will be determined by the context.

1. The horse symbolizes fortitude and confidence, as per Clement's *Stromata Book V*, Chapter VII:

> *"The horse symbolizes fortitude and confidence"*

2. Horse is the hieroglyphic symbol for Noble.

The horse represents the driving force that when directed correctly will lead to nobility.

3. Exceptional people are KNIGHTED by the monarch.

This Egyptian concept is found in present traditions when, because of a person's extraordinary accomplishments, they are KNIGHTED by no other person but the Monarch.

4. Depicted defeating forces of chaos.

The divine man is depicted on Egyptian temples as charging and defeating chaotic forces, represented as foreigners and wild animals.

These depictions are symbolic representations of the inner battle within, between the forces of Good and Evil.

In mundane sense, riding police everywhere use horses to guide and control crowds. Horse power is also used by police to dissipate disorderly crowds.

We use the term Horse Power as a measure of energy.

5. In Egyptian traditions the human tongue is equated to a horse. The tongue is the strongest muscle in the human body. The driving force of the horse or tongue control your destiny.

The symbolism of the horse as the driving force is very powerful, indeed.

Ibis [G 25 – 30]

Various attributes are all related to the ibis. The specific attribute will be determined by the context.

There are several hieroglyphic symbols for the ibis which are indicative of various types and positions.

1. The ibis represents the universal lunar principle, as per Clement's *Stromata, Book V*, Chapter VII:

> *"...the ibis, of the moon, likening the shady parts to that which is dark in plumage, and the luminous to the light.*

2. The ibis signifies the ecliptic, as per Clement's *Stromata, Book V*, Chapter VII:

> *"the ibis signifies the ecliptic. For the ibis seems, above other animals, to have furnished to the Egyptians the first rudiments of the invention of number and measure, as the oblique line did of circles."*

3. The ibis is closely associated with Thoth; also being of the lunar principle.

4. The Ibis is associated with the Equilateral triangle, as per Plutarch, in his *Moralia Volume V,* about Ancient Egypt, who wrote:

"By the spreading of Ibis' feet, in their relation to each other and to her bill, she makes an equilateral triangle."

Lion & Lioness [E 22-23]

Various attributes are all related to the lions. The specific attribute will be determined by the context.

There are several hieroglyphic symbols for the lions which are indicative of various types and positions.

[E 22—striding lion] [E 23—crouching/recumbent/sitting lion—defensive role]

1. The lion symbolizes strength, majesty, power, dominion, etc. Clement of Alexandria, in his *Stromata, Book V,* Chapter VII, wrote:

"The lion is for the Egyptians is the symbol of strength and prowess."

2. The lioness represents *'The Den Mother',* with all that implies—passionate, protective, tender, loving, caring, supportive, and encouraging.

The lioness is represented in Ancient Egypt as **SekhMut.** Sekhmet or Sekhmut is actually two words—Sekh and Mut—meaning *Elder* or *the Den Mother.*

3. The lioness represents the fiery aspect of the creative power.

In the *Litany of Re*, Re is described (in one of his 75 forms/attributes) as **The One of the Cat**, and as **The Great Cat**.

4. The lioness is the most fearless animal on Earth. In our modern societies, the guts and spine are symbols of physical courage. This concept has Ancient Egyptian roots. In the *Papyrus of Ani* [pl.32 item 42], we read:

my belly and my spine are Sekh-Mut

Pig [E 12]

As a wild animal, it represents the wild aspect of creation and therefore the wild pig is considered one of Seth' accomplices/animals.

Rams [E 10-11]

Various attributes are all related to the rams. The specific attribute will be determined by the context.

The Egyptian hieroglyphs show one type of ram, with horizontal horns. In wall depictions and statues, there are two distinct rams:

> 1. Looped horns—that refers to manifestation aspects of creation such as the zodiac Aries Age, that last began about 2300 BCE.
> 2. Horizontal horns—that refers to conceptual aspects of creation as represented by Khnum.

Our focus here will be on the hieroglyphic ram with long horizontal horns.

The ram in Ancient Egypt was called Ba.

Ba has several inter-related meanings:

   a. the vehicle of the universal spirit
   b. the embodiment of power/vital force
   c. the external manifestation of power

All of the above represents Khnum as an aspect of the creative force of Re.

Khnum represents the divine process aspect of shaping and forming the universe, both physically and metaphysically.

There are 75 forms or aspects of Re, and Khnum is one of these aspects.

Khnum represents the embodiment of the creative force of Re.

The animal in which Khnum became incarnate was the ram, with flat horns projecting at right angles to his head.

Khnum is depicted, in some context, as a ram-headed bird. This bird represents the Ba of Re—The All-Encompassing universal Ba.

Serpents [I 9-15]

Various attributes are all related to the serpents. The

specific attribute will be determined by the context as being either 'good' or 'evil'.

Various hieroglyphs are used to correspond to variations of purpose and action—repose, erect, coiled, etc. Serpents represent various aspects, such as:

1. To symbolize the dual nature of creation

The serpent represents the dualizing principle; the ability of One to divide into Two.

Looking at a serpent, it represents Unity, with its undifferentiated length.

It is Unity that contains the power that results in duality.

In pre-creation, the female aspects of pre-creation are represented as serpents, with their tails being held to represent the potential creation powers within.

The serpent, which is a remarkably individualistic animal, bears both a forked tongue (verbal duality) and a double penis (sexual duality).

The serpent, being the most flexible animal, represents the provider of all the various forms of creation.

<u>Neheb Kau</u>—meaning the provider of forms/attributes/qualities—was the name given to the serpent representing the primordial serpent/spiral in Ancient Egypt.

Neheb Kau is depicted as a two-headed serpent, indicative of the dual spiral nature of the universe.

2. To symbolize divine intellect

As a symbol of duality, the serpent represents intellect, the faculty by which man can break down the whole into its constituent parts. This is analogous to creation in the sense that multiplicity is created out of unity.

3. Symbol of potency of creation

The ability to multiply is a female aspect. As such, the form of a serpent was the hieroglyphic symbol used to represent a *netert* (goddess). The female aspect, the *netert* (goddess), represents the active potent power in the universe.

4. The Power of Opposition ["Evil"]

The creation cycle dictate that the multiplicity will be reunited into its original unity again. To achieve reunification the dualizing nature symbolized by the serpent must be resisted.

Apep (Apopis) is a coiled serpent—a form of Seth, representing the power of opposition to resurrection.

Vulture [G 14-16]

Various attributes are all related to the vultures. The specific attribute will be determined by the context.

1. The vulture represents barrenness.

2. The vulture is a symbol of **virgin birth**—in other words, **purity**. The vulture expresses the concept of 'Virgin Birth' because the female vulture gets impregnated by exposing herself to the spray of a male, without any bodily contact.

The most prominent example is that of The Virgin Mother Isis and her Child Horus—Madonna and the Child.

3. The vulture represents Mut the assimilative power with all that implies.

4. The vulture is supposed to be particularly zealous in caring for its young.

CHAPTER 5 : HUMAN AND ANIMAL-HEADED HUMAN HIEROGLYPHIC IMAGES

5.1 METAPHYSICAL SIGNIFICANCE OF HUMAN IMAGES

So many phrases are being used throughout the world, which consistently state that the human being is made in the image of God, i.e. is a miniature universe; and that to understand the universe is to understand oneself, and vice versa.

Yet, no culture has ever practiced this principle like the Ancient Egyptians. Central to their complete understanding of the universe was the knowledge that man was made in the image of God, and as such, man represented the image of all creation.

Human Egyptian-related hieroglyphic images are found in sections A & B of the standard *List of Hieroglyphics* [available on the internet].

5.2 METAPHYSICAL SIGNIFICANCE OF ANIMAL HEADED IMAGES

As stated earlier, the Egyptians' careful observation and

profound knowledge of the natural world enabled them to identify certain animals with specific qualities that could symbolize certain divine functions and principles in a particularly pure and striking fashion. As such, certain animals were chosen as symbols for that particular aspect of divinity. When a total animal is presented in Ancient Egypt, it represents a particular function/attribute in its purest form. When an animal-headed figure/image is presented, it conveys that particular function/attribute in the universe—being depicted in human form—consistent with the theme that man is the image of the whole of creation.

The animal-headed human images represent the divine forces which the Egyptian called Neteru (gods, goddesses). They are manifestations of the divine energy in the universe.

In order for creation to exist and to be maintained, this divine energy must be thought of in terms of male and female principles. Therefore, Ancient Egyptians expressed the cosmic energy forces in the terms of *netert* (female principle) and *neter* (male principle).

[For more detailed about the cosmic functions of the *neteru* (gods, goddesses), read other publications by same author, specially *Egyptian Cosmology* and *Egyptian Divinities*.]

5.3 SAMPLE RELATED EGYPTIAN HIEROGLYPHIC IMAGES

Next are selected Egyptian hieroglyphic images with human and animal-headed human-related pictographs, with a very brief review of each's metaphysical functions/attributes. It is always helpful to think of 'figures of speech' related to each image in order to recognize each's nature/behavior/characteristics/attributes.

The primary function of these Egyptian ideograms is to represent thoughts. This means that one must be searching for both the Figurative (an object stands for one of its qualities) and the Allegorical (an object is linked through enigmatic conceptual processes).

We must always keep in mind the relationships between visual forms and their meaning. A visual form may be mimetic or imitative, directly copying features of the object it represents; it may be associative, suggesting attributes which are not visually present such as abstract properties incapable of literal depiction; and finally, it may be symbolic, meaningful only when decoded according to conventions or systems of knowledge which, though not inherently visual, are communicated through visual means.

Human and animal-headed human-related Egyptian hieroglyphic images are found in sections A, B & C of the standard *List of Hieroglyphics*.

<u>Aged man with stick</u> [A 19-20]

In his *Moralia, Vol. V*, Plutarch states:

> "*the aged man* [in the Egyptian hieroglyphs] *is the symbol of departing from it—*"

Clement of Alexandria, in his *Stromata, Book V*, Chapter VII, wrote:

"an old man [in the Egyptian hieroglyphs]*is the symbol of decay."*

Bound Arms [A 13]

As always, we should look at a figure of speech setting — *'my hands/arms are tied'*. This hieroglyphic image represents the inability to act—harmless—neutralized—under control—etc.

Child—Inquiring [A 2, 17, 18]

An index finger held to the mouth represents feeding knowledge—a state of the development progression. Clement of Alexandria, in his *Stromata, Book V*, Chapter VII, wrote:

"a boy [in the Egyptian hieroglyphs]*is the symbol of production"*

Man with a Stick [A 21-26]

A man with a stick has many meanings, depending on the position of the stick and the context.

The stick represents the concept of negation, with all that it implies.

Keep in mind examples of similar, figurative uses of the word 'stick' in the English language, such as:

'Stick it (to him, etc.)'—'Nothing to shake a stick at'— 'a carrot and a stick'

Seated with no seat [A 17-18]

The seat gives legitimacy and authority—like a throne.

The absence of a seat has the opposite meaning.

Seated on a seat [A 50-51]

The seat gives legitimacy and authority—like a throne.

Also see the 'Seat' hieroglyphic symbol in Chapter 8 of this book.

Shepherd [seated *neter/netert* (gods/goddesses)] [A 40-49, B 1-7, 9-10, 12, 17]

Shepherd represents the divinity in man.

Each shepherd figure represents a specific aspect/role/concept in the creation process and its governance.

For more detailed information see *Egyptian Cosmology* and *Egyptian Divinities* by Moustafa Gadalla.

Woman and child [B 5-6]

The Madonna and child have been present in Ancient Egypt since its very remote history, for it is the allegory of The Egyptian Virgin Mother Isis and her child Horus. As such, this symbol is loaded with meanings centered around creation itself.

Much more information about Deities can be found in the book *Egyptian Divinities* by Moustafa Gadalla.

CHAPTER 6 : HUMAN BODY PARTS HIEROGLYPHIC IMAGES

6.1 METAPHYSICAL SIGNIFICANCE OF HUMAN BODY PARTS IMAGES

It is a human instinct worldwide to use a human organ/part to describe a metaphysical aspect. The Ancient Egyptian texts and symbols are permeated with this complete understanding that the man (whole and parts) is the image of the universe (whole and parts).

For Ancient Egyptians, man, as a miniature universe, represents the created images of all creation. Since Re—the cosmic creative impulse—is called *"The One Joined together, Who Comes Out of His Own Members"*, so the human being (the image of creation) is, likewise, A *One Joined Together*. The human body is a unity that consists of different parts, joined together. In the *Litany of Re*, the body parts of the divine man are each identified with a neter/netert (god/goddess).

If man is the universe in miniature, then all factors in man are duplicated on a greater scale in the universe. All drives and forces which are powerful in man are also powerful in the universe at large. In accordance with the Egyptians' cosmic consciousness, every action performed by man is believed to be linked to a greater pattern in the universe, including sneezing, blinking, spitting, shouting, weeping, dancing, playing, eating, drinking, and sexual intercourse.

Man, to the Ancient Egyptians, was the embodiment of the laws of creation. As such, the physiological functions and processes of the various parts of the body were seen as manifestations of cosmic functions. The limbs and organs had a metaphysical function, in addition to their physical purpose. The parts of the body were consecrated to one of the neteru (divine principles), which appeared in the Egyptian records throughout its recovered history. In addition to the *Litany of Re*, here are other examples:

Utterance 215 § 148-149, from the *Sarcophagus Chamber of Unas' Tomb* (rubble pyramid) at Saqqara, identifies the parts of the body (head, nose, teeth, arms, legs, etc.), each with the divine *neteru*.

> **Thy head is that of Horus**
> ...
> **thy nose is a Anubis**
> **thy teeth are Sopdu**
> **thy arms are Happy and Dua-mutef,**
> ...
> **thy legs are Imesty and Kebeh-senuf,**
> ...
> **All thy members are the twins of Atam.**

From the *Papyrus of Ani*, [pl. 32, item 42]:

> **My hair is Nun; my face is Re; my eyes are Hathor; my ears are Wepwawet; my nose is She who presides**

> *over her lotus-leaf; my lips are Anubis; my molars are Selket; my incisors are Isis; my arms are the Ram, the Lord of Mendes; my breast is Neith; my back is Seth; my phallus is Osiris; . . . my belly and my spine are Sekhmet; my buttocks are the Eye of Horus; my thighs and my calves are Nut; my feet are Ptah; . . . there is no member of mine devoid of a neter (god), and Thoth is the protection of all my flesh.*

The above text leaves no doubt about the divinity of each human body member:

> <u>**there is no member of mine devoid of a neter (god, goddess).**</u>

6.2 SAMPLE RELATED EGYPTIAN HIEROGLYPHIC IMAGES

Human organs and body parts related Egyptian hieroglyphic images are found in section D of the standard *List of Hieroglyphics* [available on the internet].

The primary function of these Egyptian ideograms is to represent thoughts. This means that one must be searching for both the Figurative (an object stands for one of its qualities) and the Allegorical (an object is linked through enigmatic conceptual processes).

We must always keep in mind the relationships between visual forms and their meaning. A visual form may be mimetic or imitative, directly copying features of the object it represents; it may be associative, suggesting attributes which are not visually present such as abstract properties incapable of literal depiction; and finally, it may be symbolic, meaningful only when decoded according to conventions or systems of knowledge which, though not inherently visual, are communicated through visual means.

Next are selected Egyptian hieroglyphic images with human body part-related pictographs, with a very brief review of each one's metaphysical functions/attributes. It is always helpful to think of 'figures of speech' related to each image in order to recognize each one's nature/behavior/characteristics/attributes.

Arms [D 35-45] arm and hand – [D 28] Ka

There are a number of hieroglyphic symbols showing variation of the forearm together with the hand—different positions and gestures, such as:

– 90 degrees or a bent elbow
– hands open, closed, fist, palm facing down/up—etc.

The symbol is for the whole arm (not just forearm) and the hand has many possible meanings:

1. Upper limb of the human body
2. Forearm signifies work, strength, etc.
3. Power, to seize, control: *'the long arm of the law'*
4. Force—in an earthly sense: weapons, branch of military; to equip with parts needed for operation/war; to enter a dispute

The whole metrological system in Egypt was based on the human figure, its units derived from an ideal limb length. The main standard linear measure was the cubit: the length of the forearm from elbow to tip of middle finger, further divided into 7 handbreadths/palms of four digits(fingers) each or 28 digits in total. One Egyptian cubit is 1.72' or 0.5236 m.

The Ka [**D 28**] is portrayed as a pair of arms outstretched towards heaven. The Ka is basically one of nine major metaphysical components of man. The Ka is the combination of several intertwined subcomponents. It is equated to what we describe as *personality*. The Ka does not die with the mortal body, although it may break into its many sub-components.

Ears [D 18]

Ears signify hearing and subsequent larger metaphysical senses of acknowledging, learning, and comprehending. One of the texts in the *Egyptian Book of the Caverns* describes the unilluminated:

> *"They are like this, those who do not see the Great God, who do not perceive the rays of his disk, whose souls do not leave the earth, who <u>do not hear the words of this Great God</u> when he passes near to their cavern."*

The description is very similar to the Gospel references to those with *"eyes to see and ears to hear"*.

Eye & Its Parts [D4-17]

There are several hieroglyphic images that show variations of the eye symbol [**D4-10**] and parts of the eye [**D11-17**].

1. The eye is the part of the body able to perceive the light, and is therefore a symbol for spiritual ability.

One of the texts, in the *Egyptian Book of the Caverns*, describes the unilluminated:

> *"They are like this, those <u>who do not see the Great God, who do not perceive the rays of his disk</u>, whose souls do not leave the earth, who do not hear the words of this Great God when he passes near to their cavern."*

The description is very similar to the Gospel references to those with "*eyes to see and ears to hear*".

2. The right eye symbolizes the solar principle and the left eye symbolizes the lunar principle. The two eyes together symbolize the total unity of the dual principles of creation.

3. *"The eye for the Egyptians symbolizes the watchman of justice and the guardian of the whole body"*, as quoted by Diodorus of Sicily.

<u>Parts of the eye</u> [D 11-17]—In conjunction with the whole metrological system which was based on the human figure, in Egypt, the sections of the eye are the glyphs for the fractions 1/2 to 1/64.

<u>Female Genitalia</u> [V 39]

Isis represents the female principle of nature.

Her symbol was given the names 'knot of Isis' and 'The blood of Isis', shaped as stylized female genitalia.

This female symbol is always found next to Osiris' Tet Pillar—the male phallic symbol—to signify the binary nature of life itself.

Hand and Fingers   [D 46-49] Hand [D 50-51] Fingers

Earlier in this chapter, we highlighted the metaphysically significant meanings of variation of the forearm together with the hand—different positions, gestures, etc. Our focus then was on the forearm. Here, our focus will be on the hand [D 46-49] and fingers [D 50-51].

There are a number of hieroglyphic symbols showing variations of the hand—different positions, gestures, such as hands open or closed, clenched fist, palm facing down/up, etc.

The hand symbolized/symbolizes several concepts, one of which is action, and therefore creation and latent creative power.

The hand symbolizes the female principle.

The role of the loving hand found its way into most cultures, for when a man wants to marry, he asks the girl's father for her hand.

In all ages and among all peoples, the hand has been a symbol of strength and power, and a picture of it has been regarded as a representation of God. In the Egyptian text of the *Book of Gates*, on the alabaster coffin of Seti I, the *"Great Hand"* means '*the supreme Power which rules heaven and earth*'.

A **closed hand with the first finger alone outstretched** was regarded as a sure protection against the Evil Eye.

A fist—**'tight** fist'—means compression, determination, oppression, etc. The particular meaning is determined by the context/setting of the text.

Right and Left Hand Significance—Diodorus of Sicily wrote about the metaphysical meanings of hands in Ancient Egypt:

> *"The right hand with its fingers outstretched signifies the getting of a livelihood, and the left hand drawn in on itself signifies the watching and guardianship of possessions".*

An active right hand symbolizes giving. An active left hand signifies receiving.

<u>Fingers</u> [D 50-51]—Each finger was associated with certain planetary and cosmic/natural attributes.

The thumb and its position in relation to the other four fingers is of the greatest importance. The most natural position for the newborn infant's thumb is to be closed in by the fist. This signifies an absence of any form of expression.

The thumb is the very image of being. Hiding the **thumb** is hiding potency, the essence of being. Hiding it shows a desire for protection and a dependence on other powers. It is the favorite gesture of the escapist, the resigned person who has "given up."

The opposite position to the "**thumb-closed-in-by-fist**" gesture is the thumb that stretches far out from the palm. Forming an exact right angle with the index finger, it signifies full consciousness.

This gesture is indicative of the capacity to direct and command other things.

Many **variations of thumb positions** exist between the two extreme types of the hidden thumb and the thumb in its right angle position to the index finger.

The thumb is often found in a special position relative to the four fingers when they form a fist.

The **thumb represents** intellect in contrast to the fingers, the symbolic seat of the emotions. When the thumb rests comfortably beside the clenched fingers, such a gesture signifies that "mind" dominates "emotion."

The **index finger**, next to the thumb, is the only one which displays independence of movement and a strongly demonstrative, persuasive power. The strength of this finger lies in its belonging to the motoricactive part of the hand. It is the best and most helpful assistant to the thumb. Through their collaboration, we learn to gauge volume, quantity and space, and to "handle" most of the activities which are directed by mental or physical skill.

In summary: each finger has its own characteristics and metaphysical significance—so, also, does a combination of two or more fingers.

Through the sense of touch, images are produced which heighten for us the realization of the object. Another compelling motive to touch exemplifies the direct connection of this sense with our nervous system and brain.

For information about the role of hands and fingers in music, read *The Enduring Ancient Egyptian Musical System* by Moustafa Gadalla.

Head [D 1]

The head signifies the whole being—chief—first.

When we use expressions such as *'Using our heads'*, it signifies intellect, rationale, etc.

Heart [F 34]

The heart was/is considered to be a symbol of intellectual perceptions, consciousness, and moral courage.

Both the **heart and tongue** complement each other, as stated clearly in the *Shabaka Stele* (716–701 BCE), which is a reproduction from the 3rd Dynasty:

> *"The Heart thinks all that it wishes, and the Tongue delivers all that it wishes."*

During the process of 'Judgment Day', the heart, as a metaphor for conscience, is weighed against the feather of truth, to determine the fate of the deceased.

Legs [D 54-60]

Human legs [from top of thigh down to the foot] function as both support and mobility of the upper body. Legs, as such, can signify both static/standing meanings as well as dynamic/active motion.

The leg signifies many legal aspects such as stand/standing/position, legal right/inheritance, ancestor/legendary rights, etc. Such is not limited to Egyptian culture, but is ingrained in the human nature. There are many meanings in English for words that begin with or relate to the symbolic meanings of the leg:

- *'no leg to stand on'*
- *'put foot in the door'*
- *'take a foothold'*
- *'kick out habit/someone'*
- *'Put foot down'* – firmness/determination/final

The hieroglyphic symbols for human legs come in three basic categories:

1. Two walking legs [motion]—[D 54-55]

represents ability to come, go, forward, backward, etc.

2. A lower leg [vertical] with a bent thigh—[D 56-57]

– represents movement

– Bending knees = motion is possible.
– Bending—with knife = unbending—no trespassing—with all that it implies.

3. **A lower leg [vertical] without thigh [foot]—[D 58-60]**

– unbending [knees] no motion—stay put = position, etc.

Mouth [D 21] mouth [D 22] 2/3 sign

The hieroglyphic sign known as the "mouth of Re" denotes unity.

In conjunction with the whole metrological system in Egypt that was based on the human figure, a fraction—any fraction—could only be a fraction of unity. Esoterically, because all numbers are to be regarded as divisions of unity, the mathematical relationship a number bears to unity is a key to its nature.

The Ancient Egyptians represented fractions – i.e. having a numerator of 1 – by drawing the mouth of Re as the numerator and unit marks underneath for the denominator.

The "mouth" sign signifies the fraction sign—the ratio of 1 (whole) to the part (fraction).

To write $1/7^{th}$, the Egyptian simply wrote the numeral 7 in an upside-down form underneath the mouth of Re's symbol.

A seventh is called Re-Sefhet = *'mouth of seven'*. The glyph might be translated as *'One emits seven'*.

In Ancient Egypt, the words of Re, revealed through Thoth, became the parts (fractions) of the world.

The Egyptian texts state that the created universe came out of the mouth (of Re), and the mouth is the symbol of Unity—the One—in hieroglyphs.

Phallus [D 52-53]

An erect phallus represents the power of generation, or the reproductive force of nature. To depict the concept of fertility in a visual form is the obvious choice.

CHAPTER 7 : NATURE AND GEOMETRICAL FIGURE HIEROGLYPHIC IMAGES

7.1 SAMPLE RELATED EGYPTIAN HIEROGLYPHIC IMAGES

The primary function of these Egyptian ideograms is to represent thoughts. This means that one must be searching for both the Figurative (an object stands for one of its qualities) and the Allegorical (an object is linked through enigmatic conceptual processes).

We must always keep in mind the relationships between visual forms and their meaning. A visual form may be mimetic or imitative, directly copying features of the object it represents; it may be associative, suggesting attributes which are not visually present such as abstract properties incapable of literal depiction; and finally, it may be symbolic, meaningful only when decoded according to conventions or systems of knowledge which, though not inherently visual, are communicated through visual means.

Nature and uncategorized geometrical figures related to Egyptian hieroglyphic images are found in sections

M N O V W X Z Aa of the standard *List of Hieroglyphics* [available on the internet].

Next are selected Egyptian hieroglyphic images with nature and geometrically related pictographs, with a very brief review of each's metaphysical functions/attributes. It is always helpful to think of 'figures of speech' related to each image in order to recognize each one's nature/behavior/characteristics/attributes.

Buds—(Open & Closed) [M 8 15 16]

Referred to—mistakenly—as *lotus and papyrus plants*. They had nothing to do with lotus and papyrus plants, since both forms are shown, alternating, in all depictions of marshes, etc.

It is not two plants but a single plant with open and closed forms (being the Egyptian water lily that closes at night and sinks under water, to rise and open again at dawn). It was a natural symbol of the sun and of creation.

The closed form represents the metaphysical—hidden—unmanifested state.

The open form represents the physical—the manifested.

The open bud form always relates to renewal and rebirth—as is the case with Nefer-Tum. The Ancient Egyptian texts describe Nefer-Tum as being born anew each morning from the lily.

As far back as 4,400 years ago, we read, in the commonly known *Pyramid Texts* addressing the Pharaoh Unas:

> *"Rise like Nefer Tem from the lily and to come forth on the horizon every day".*

Nefer-Tum rises out of an open bud—renewal—rebirth.

Circle & parts of

A circle, portions/segments and variations thereof are found in many hieroglyphic symbols. Here we will deal with the metaphysical significance of:

1. the full circle
2. top half circle
3. Neb sign

1. *A Circle with a dot or point in the center* [N -33]

The cosmic creative force, Re, is written as a circle with a dot or point in the center.

It is a circle moving in a circle, one and solitary. The circle symbolically represents the Absolute, or undifferentiated Unity. The circle, appropriately enough, is the universal archetype of creation.

2. *Top half circle* [X 1]

The top half of the archetypal circle represents the physical manifestation of creation.

3. *Neb sign* [O 30]

Neb is an Ancient Egyptian term meaning gold (traditionally, the finished perfected end product, the goal of the alchemist), Lord, master, all, affirmation, and pure.

The hieroglyph denoting Neb is a segment of a circle, whose central angle is 140 degrees. The ratio of this angle to the whole circle (length of the arc to the whole circumference) = 0.3889, which constitutes the second power of 0.625. The second power spiritually constitutes reaching to a higher level. Neb means exactly that.

The ratio 0.625 was used in Ancient Egyptian design as the ratio of 5:8, and such numbers [5 and 8] are important numbers in the Summation (so-called Fibonacci) Series as well as in the Neb (Golden) Proportion.

Sky/firmament [N 1]

The firmament known as heaven is described in Ancient Egypt as the sky viewed poetically as a solid arch or vault. The ancient Egyptian texts describe Isis as:

> *Queen of heaven*
>
> *Queen of the Firmament*

In her role as the firmament, Isis is recognized as Nut, representing the heavens as a physical ceiling the vault of heavens.

Spiral [Z 7]

Spirals—alone or incorporated into other forms—are one of the most utilized Ancient Egyptian hieroglyphs.

The abundant use of spirals in Ancient Egypt is indicative of their representations of all growth patterns in the universe.

The spiral in nature is the result of continued proportional growth. This type of spiral is known mathematically as the constant angle or logarithmic spiral. Logarithmic expansion is the basis for the geometry of spirals. The fetus of man and animals, which are the manifestation of the generation laws, are shaped like the logarithmic spiral. Manifestations of spirals are evident in vegetable and shell growth, spider webs, the horn of the dall sheep, the trajectory of many subatomic particles, the nuclear force of atoms, the double helix of DNA, and most of all, in many of the galaxies. Patterns in the mental realm, as well, are also generated in spiraling motions.

We find the logarithmic spiral shown on the red crown of Ancient Egypt. This crown represents the solar (in broader terms than just the sun) principle that is the generative matrix that is called Re.

We also find it in the coiled body of a cobra representing the divine female principle—Netert (goddess)—representing the active potent power in the universe.

Star [N 14-15]

The Egyptian five-pointed star forms the corners of

the pentagon which is harmoniously inscribed in the Sacred Circle of Re. The Star was the Egyptian symbol for both destiny and the number five. The five pointed stars were the homes of departed souls, as stated in the *Unas* (wrongly known as Pyramid) *Texts*, Line 904:

> *"be a soul as a living star."*

Sun and Moon [Solar and Lunar Principles] [N 5-12]

Several hieroglyphic symbols [N 5-12] are depicted to represent the solar and lunar principles and their corresponding interplay/relationships, as manifested in the sun and moon.

For the Egyptians the sun and moon provide more than light during the day and night times. Their significant roles were explained by Diodorus of Sicily in his *Book I*, [11. 5-6]:

> *"These two neteru (gods)—Isis and Osiris—they hold, regulate the entire universe, giving both nourishment and increase to all things....*

Then Diodorus explains the Ancient Egyptian reasoning for the significance of the sun and moon on the universal existence, as follows:

> *"Moreover, practically all the physical matter which is essential to the generation of all things is furnished by these two neteru (gods), Isis and Osiris, symbolized as the sun and the moon. The sun contributing the fiery element and the spirit, the moon the wet and the dry, and both together*

the air; and it is through these elements that all things are engendered and nourished.

And so it is out of the sun and moon that the whole physical body of the universe is made complete; and as for the five parts just named of these bodies—the spirit, the fire, the dry, as well as the wet, and, lastly, the air—just as in the case of a man we enumerate head and hands and feet and the other parts, so in the same way the body of the universe is composed in its entirety of these parts."

Triangles [Various Forms]

There are several forms of triangles to be found in Egyptian hieroglyphs.

For the Ancient Egyptians, Three/Triads/Trinities/Triangles are one and the same. There was no difference between geometric triangles, musical triads, or any of the numerous trinities of Ancient Egypt. The physical and metaphysical role of Three is recognized in the many trinities of Ancient Egypt.

The best example was explained by Plutarch regarding the 3:4:5 triangle. Plutarch stated in *Moralia Vol. V*:

> *"The Egyptians hold in high honor the most beautiful of the triangles, since they liken the nature of the Universe most closely to it..."*

In other words, triangles in their different forms represent different natures in the universe.

The 3:4:5 triangle, where the height is to the base as 3 is to 4, was called the "Osiris Triangle" by Plutarch. It is a historical lie to call it the Pythagorean Triangle. It was used in Ancient Egypt for thousands of years before Pythagoras walked this earth. It is very clear from Plutarch's testimony below, that the ancient Egyptians knew that 3:4:5 is a right-angle triangle, since 3 is called upright and 4 is the base, forming a 90-degree angle.

Plutarch wrote about the 3:4:5 right-angle triangle of Ancient Egypt in *Moralia Vol. V*:

> *"The Egyptians hold in high honor the most beautiful of the triangles, since they liken the nature of the Universe most closely to it, as Plato in the Republic seems to have made use of it in formulating his figure of marriage.*
>
> *This triangle has its upright of three units, its base of four, and its hypotenuse of five, whose power is equal to that of the other two sides. The upright, therefore, may be likened to the male, the base to the female, and the hypotenuse to the child of both, and so Osiris may be regarded as the origin, Isis as the recipient, and Horus as perfected result. Three is the first perfect odd number: four is a square whose side is the even number two; but five is in some ways like to its father, and in some ways like to its mother, being made up of three and two. And panta (all) is a derivative of pente (five), and they speak of counting as "numbering by fives. Five makes a square of itself."*

The vitality and the interactions between these numbers show how they are male and female, active and passive, vertical and horizontal... etc.

In the animated world of Ancient Egypt, numbers did not simply designate quantities but instead were considered to be concrete definitions of energetic formative principles of nature. The Egyptians called these energetic principles neteru (gods, goddesses).

In addition to the 3:4:5 triangle, we also have a specific reference to the equilateral triangle.

Plutarch, in his *Moralia Vol. V* about Ancient Egypt, wrote:

> **By the spreading of Ibis' feet, in their relation to each other and to her bill, she makes an equilateral triangle.**

Ibis is the sacred bird of Thoth, whose words created the world.

Trees [M 1]

The tree symbolizes ALL aspects of the creation cycle—both the emanation of the original unity as well as the eventual return of all things back to the original unity.

The Tree of Life links the heavens, the earth, and all that is hidden and growing below.

There are several types of trees each with its own metaphysical significance:

1. The Egyptians believed that certain deities took up their abode in trees, and several trees were regarded by them as sacred.

The most significant female Tree deity is Hathor.

About the significance of Hathor's tree, Plutarch, in *Moralia Vol. V* (378,68 G), states:

> *"Of the plants in Egypt they say that the persea is especially consecrated to the goddess (Hathor) because its fruit resembles a heart and its leaf a tongue".*

The universal rule of cause and effect—symbolized by the functions of the heart and tongue—is found on the *Egyptian Shabaka Stele* (716-701 BCE), as follows:

> *"The Heart and the Tongue have power over all... the neteru* (gods, goddesses), *all men, all cattle, all creeping things, and all that lives. The Heart thinks all that it wishes, and the Tongue delivers all that it wishes.*

The combined role of the heart and the tongue is extended in all aspects of Ancient Egypt existence.

2. The successful soul will achieve immortality and will be enshrined in the Tree of Life.

We read about the significance of the immortal Tree of Life as far back as The Egyptian Pharaoh Pepi more than 4,300 years ago. The text in chapter 20 in his tomb reads:

> *"This Pepi travelleth to the Great Lake in Sekhet-hetep, by which the Great Gods alight, and these great ones of the imperishable stars <u>give unto Pepi the tree of life whereon they themselves do live, so that he also may live thereon</u>."*

<u>Water surface</u> [N 35]

Water is the source of life and reanimation as well as of cleansing—purification.

A water surface [N 35] signifies a level of consciousness. A new/raised consciousness is equivalent to a new awakening. In Sufi traditions, each level of consciousness is referred to as death—rebirth. The same thinking has pervaded Ancient (and present-day) Egypt, where birth and rebirth is a constant theme. The word death is employed in a figurative sense. The theme that man must "die before he dies" or that he must be "born again" in his present life is taken symbolically, or is commemorated by a ritual. In this, the candidate has to pass through certain specific experiences (technically termed "deaths"). A good example is baptism, which was the main objective at Easter, after Lent—representing death of the old self by immersing into water, and the rising of the new/renewed self by coming out of the water.

Three water surfaces [N 35] signifies the three levels of consciousness associated with Thoth.

The three levels of consciousness in the Egyptian mystical traditions are:

1. The purification process of body and soul.
2. Gaining knowledge through both intellect and intuition (revelation).
3. Vanishing into the Divine Essence through the cessation of all conscious thought.

For more details read *Egyptian Mystics: Seekers of The Way* by this same author.

For more information about the metaphysical aspects of geometrical forms and sacred geometry, read *Ancient Egyptian Metaphysical Architecture* by Moustafa Gadalla.

CHAPTER 8 : MAN MADE OBJECT HIEROGLYPHIC IMAGES

8.1 METAPHYSICAL SIGNIFICANCE OF MAN MADE OBJECTS IMAGES

Imitation through imagination means the creation of carefully designed objects, to be set beside the natural objects of the world. The method of artistic creation and the shape of the object created are the specifically human realizations of the universal creative forces present in nature. It is the force of the imagination through which we can feel ourselves related sympathetically to the larger, "latent" force of the cosmos. In creating new objects with the aid of the imagination, the mystic does not desert reality by constructing things alien and unnatural. Imagination does not tamper with the world but moves it in accordance with nature.

Guided by the principles of sacred geometry [and its cosmic origin], the Egyptian man made objects represent metaphysical thoughts and concepts.

In Egyptian symbolism, the precise role/function or functions of the neteru (gods/goddesses) or earthly humans are revealed in many ways by manmade objects such as dress, headdress, crown, color, sacred object (e.g., flail, scepter, staff, ankh), etc. This symbolic language represents a wealth of physical, physiological, psychological and spiritual data in the presented symbols.

8.2 SAMPLE RELATED EGYPTIAN HIEROGLYPHIC IMAGES

The primary function of these Egyptian ideograms is to represent thoughts. This means that one must be searching for both the Figurative (an object stands for one of its qualities) and the Allegorical (an object is linked through enigmatic conceptual processes).

We must always keep in mind the relations between visual forms and their meaning. A visual form may be mimetic or imitative, directly copying features of the object it represents; it may be associative, suggesting attributes which are not visually present such as abstract properties incapable of literal depiction; and finally, it may be symbolic, meaningful only when decoded according to conventions or systems of knowledge which, though not inherently visual, are communicated through visual means.

Nature and uncategorized geometrical figures related Egyptian hieroglyphic images are found in sections **O-Y** [Emblems, Buildings, etc.] of the standard *List of Hieroglyphics* [available on the internet].

Next are a selected Egyptian hieroglyphic images with manmade objects related pictographs, with a very brief review of each's metaphysical functions/attributes. It is always helpful to think of 'figures of speech' related to each image in order to recognize each one's nature/behavior/characteristics/attributes.

Ankh [S 34]

Represents eternal life.

Ark [P 1-4]

The sacred ark (boat) in Egyptian traditions symbolizes the power of self-renewal. The boat is qualified as a "divine being and savior from the death".

The divine ark (boat) was often called wts nfrw, *"the one who raises on high the beauty (of the neter)"*.

A small model of an ark/boat is always found in Egyptian temples and folk-saints' shrines. The ark/boat was/is called the *'ferryboat'*. The boat, with a sort of canopy, is placed on its frame prior to beginning the processions, and holds an effigy or sacred object related to the venerated deity/saint.

In Ancient Egypt, several divine arks (boats) participated in the processions. The ark stood on a pedestal in the Holy of Holies in the temple or the various shrines, and was drawn in procession by the priests on festive occasions.

Ax [T 7]

The ax is better understood in its verb form—shape, split, cut, terminate or separate/differentiate, etc.

Bed [A 55]

Throughout the Egyptian history, we find a consistent shape of depicted beds/biers in tombs and temples as being in a lion-shaped form.

The bed/bier represented death and resurrection.

Osiris symbolizes death and resurrection.

One of Osiris' titles was *The Lion*.

The Egyptian word for a lion is **SaBA.**, which is the same word for the number seven.

The universal cyclical number par excellence is SEVEN—and Osiris represents the cyclical aspect of the universe.

Osiris relates to the number seven and its multiples.

Since Osiris represents the latent power of resurrection to begin a new cycle, the Egyptians depicted the death bed in the shape of a lion—being number seven—being Osiris.

Since all people—male and females, rich and poor—are Osiris upon their death, their DEATH Bed (so to speak) represents the lion—the number seven; the Return to the Source.

Crook [S 38]

One of Osiris emblems representing the shepherd of mankind—with all that implies.

Crowns [S 1-9]

Crowns, like those of human heads represent the ability to differentiate and act. The red crown represents the solar (in broader terms than just the sun) principle that is the generative matrix. The white crown represents the lunar principle.

Farming Tools [U 1-8]

Farming tools [and scenes] have deep meaning, just like when we read parallels in the biblical parable *"Whatsoever a man soweth, that shall he also reap".* It will be silly to view it as "agricultural advice" and not for what it is—a spiritual message.

The metaphor of farming is most profound. It is the ideal of work ethics and behavioral conduct.

Flail [S 45]

Symbolizes the ability to separate wheat from chaf—metaphysically.

Knife [T 30]

To cut/halt/forbid/avoid/boycott (boy-**cut**)

Knots Tying [several forms in Section V of the standard Egyptian Hieroglyphics inventory]

The Ancient Egyptian monuments show several variations of tying the knot.

Tying the knot, in its various applications, symbolizes the reunification of the dual nature of the created universe.

Ropes—Twisted

See knot tying above.

Scale [U 38]

Several possible meanings such as: justice, harmony, balance, sage (wisdom), etc.

Scepter [S 42]

Symbolizes supremacy—mind over matter.

Seat [Q 1]

The seat is identified with Isis as the legitimate source of authority.

Such meaning is found everywhere, i.e. Seat of government, CHAIRman; etc.

Isis, in Egyptian, means seat/throne, which symbolizes the matrilineal/matriarchal principle of the Ancient Egyptian society. Isis is always shown wearing a throne upon her head. As such, Isis represents the principle of legitimacy—the actual physical throne.

Isis is the seat who gives her husband Osiris the divine power to rule. Osiris is written with the glyph of the throne and the eye, combining the concepts of legitimacy and divinity.

Tet Pillar [R 11]

The Tet pillar is an "upside-down" tree of life, emanating from the source. It is the symbol of Osiris the Divine, who came to Earth and then went back to heaven.

The Tet pillar is the spinal column of creation, which is associated with Osiris as his sacred symbol. The more significant element of the Tet is the spinal aspect of the neuro-network of life, in humans and in trees.

The 7 centers of Tet Pillar represent the 7 metaphorical rungs of the ladder, leading from matter to spirit. Since man is a microcosm of the cosmic pattern, Tet represents a microcosm of the universal cosmology.

The Tet pillar represents the lopped trunk of a cedar tree, symbolizing the possibility of renewed life.

The symbolic erection of the Tet Pillar represents the essence of the Pillar as symbol of stability.

Since the Tet Pillar represents renewed life, it almost always appears, together with the Isis symbol, in all tombs and most, if not all, temples. Her symbol was called Thet, which sounds very similar to Tet, being the symbol for Osiris.

In addition to the obvious phallic aspect of the Tet Pillar, Tet represents the sacrum of Osiris, i.e. the part of the back which is close to the sperm duct (for it symbolized the seed of Osiris). It was natural, then, to depict the genital organs of Isis as a companion amulet, for by the two amulets, the procreative powers of man and women would be symbolized.

Was Scepter [S 40]

Represents power, dominion, authority – i.e. total self-control.

Wine Press [M 43]

Wine and grape scenes signify spiritualization.

The walls of the Ancient Egyptian tombs show vintners pressing new wine, and wine-making is everywhere as a constant metaphor of spiritual processes and the themes of transformation and inner power.

The wine-making process of growing, harvesting, pressing, and fermenting is a metaphor for spiritual processes.

In Egyptian texts, Osiris was characterized as The Vine.

The soul, or the portion of its god within, causes the divine ferment in the body of life. It's developed there, as on the vine, by the sun of man's spiritual self. The fermented potency of wine was, at its deepest spiritual level, a symbol of the presence of the incarnated god within the spiritually aware person.

SELECTED BIBLIOGRAPHY

Baines, John and Jaromir Málek. *Atlas of Ancient Egypt*. New York, 1994.

Breasted, James Henry. *Ancient Records of Egypt,* 3 Vols. Chicago, USA, 1927.

Budge, E.A. Wallis. *Amulets and Superstitions*. New York, 1978.

Budge, E.A. Wallis. *Cleopatra's Needles and Other Egyptian Obelisks*. London, 1926.

Budge, E.A. Wallis. *The Decrees of Memphis and Canopis,* 3 Vols. London, 1904.

Budge, Sir E. A. Wallis. *Egyptian Language: Easy Lessons in Egyptian Hieroglyphics*. New York, 1983.

Budge, E.A. Wallis. *Egyptian Magic*. New York, 1971.

Budge, E.A. Wallis. *Egyptian Religion: Egyptian Ideas of the Future Life*. London, 1975.

Budge, E.A. Wallis. *From Fetish to God in Ancient Egypt*. London, 1934.

Budge, E.A. Wallis. *The Gods of the Egyptians,* 2 Vols. New York, 1969.

Budge, Wallis. *Osiris & The Egyptian Resurrection,* 2 Vols. New York, 1973.

Clement. *Stromata Book V,* chapter IV [www.piney.com/Clement-Stromata-Five.html]

Davies, W.V. *Egyptian Hieroglyphs.* London, 1989.

Diodorus of Sicily. *Books I, II, & IV.* Tr. By C.H. Oldfather. London, 1964.

Drucker, Johanna. *The Alphabetic Labyrinth.* New York, 1995.

Egyptian Book of the Dead (The Book of Going Forth by Day), The Papyrus of Ani. USA, 1991.

Erman, Adolf. *Life in Ancient Egypt.* New York, 1971.

Findlen, Paula, ed. *Athanasius Kircher: The Last Man Who Knew Everything.* New York, 2004.

Gadalla, Moustafa:
 – *Ancient Egyptian Culture Revealed.* USA, 2007.
 – *Egyptian Cosmology: The Animated Universe.* 2nd ed. USA, 2001.
 – *Egyptian Divinities: The All Who Are THE ONE.* USA, 2001.
 – *Egyptian Harmony: The Visual Music.* USA, 2000.
 – *Egyptian Mystics: Seekers of the Way.* USA, 2003.

Gardiner, Sir Alan. *Egyptian Grammar: Being an Introduction to the Study of Hieroglyphs,* 3rd ed. Oxford, 1994.

Gefin, Laszlo. *Ideogram: History of Poetic Method.* Austin, TX, USA, 1982.

Gelb, I.J. *A Study of Writing: The Foundation of Grammatology*. Chicago, IL, USA, 1952.

Gilsenan, Michael. *Saint and Sufi in Modern Egypt*. Oxford, 1973.

Godwin, Joscelyn. *Athanasius Kircher: A Renaissance Man and the Quest for Lost Knowledge*. London, 1979.

Helfman, Elizabeth S. *Signs and Symbols Around the World*. New York, 1967.

Herodotus. *The Histories*. Tr. By Aubrey DeSelincourt. London, 1996.

Horapollo. *The Hieroglyphics of Horapollo*. Tr. By George Boas. New York, 1950.

Iversen, Eric. *The Myth of Egypt and its Hieroglyphs*. Copenhagen, 1961.

Jensen, Hans. *Sign, Symbol and Script*. London, 1970.

Kircher, Athanasius. *Oedipus Aegyptiacus,* 3 Vols. Rome, 1652-4.

Maxwell-Stuart, P.G., ed. *The Occult in Early Modern Europe*. New York, USA, 1999.

Piankoff, Alexandre. *The Tomb of Ramesses VI*. New York, 1954.

Piankoff, Alexandre. *Mythological Papyri*. New York, 1957.

Piankoff, Alexandre. *The Litany of Re*. New York, 1964.

Piankoff, Alexandre. *The Pyramid of Unas Texts*. Princeton, NJ, USA, 1968.

Piankoff, Alexandre. *The Shrines of Tut-Ankh-Amon Texts*. New York, 1955.

Plato. *The Collected Dialogues of Plato including the Letters*. Edited by E. Hamilton & H. Cairns. New York, 1961.

Plotinus. *The Enneads, in 6 Volumes*. Tr. By A.H. Armstrong. London, 1978.

Plotinus. *The Enneads*. Tr. By Stephen MacKenna. London, 1991.

Plutarch. *De Iside Et Osiride*. Tr. By J. Gwyn Griffiths. Wales, UK, 1970.

Plutarch. *Plutarch's Moralia, Volume V*. Tr. by Frank Cole Babbitt. London, 1927.

Pritchard, James B., ed. *Ancient Near Eastern Texts*. Princeton, NJ, USA, 1955.

Shafer, Byron E. ed. *Religion in Ancient Egypt*. Ithaca, NY, USA, 1991.

Sicilus, Diodorus. *Vol 1*. Tr. by C.H. Oldfather. London, 1964.

Silverman, David and Torode, Brian. *The Material Word: Some Theories of Language and its Limits*. London, 1980.

Wilkins, John. *Mercury or the Secret and Swift Messenger*. London, 1641.

Wilkinson, Richard H. *Reading Egyptian Art*. New York, 1994.

Wilkinson, Richard H. *Symbol & Magic in Egyptian Art*. New York, 1994.

Several Internet sources.

Numerous references in Arabic language.

SOURCES AND NOTES

References to sources in the previous section, Selected Bibliography are only referred to for facts, events, and dates—not for their interpretations of such information.

It should be noted that if a reference is made to one of the author Moustafa Gadalla's books, that each of his book contains appendices for its own extensive bibliography as well as detailed Sources and Notes.

Chapter 1. Historical Deception of the (Ancient) Egyptian Linguistics

    1.1 The Imagery and Alphabetical Writing Modes—Gadalla [Culture], Petrie, Gardiner [Egyptian Grammar], Silver, Wittgenstein
    1.2 The Universal Pictorial Signs—Helfman
    1.3 The Egyptian Pictorial Metaphysical Images/Script—Gadalla [Culture, Harmony], Plutarch, Diodorus, Clement, Plotinus [Armstrong], Iverson

Chapter 2. The Scientific/Metaphysical Realities of Pictorial Images (Hieroglyphs)

    2.1 Images: Language Of The Mind/Consciousness/Divine—Silver [Kafka], Khaldun, Gefin,

Pritchard [*Shabaka Stele*]

2.2 The Soundness of The Three Roles of Each Egyptian Hieroglyphic Image—Horapollo, Iverson, Clement, Silver [Wittgenstein & Kafka], Drucker, Freud, Gadalla [Divinities, Cosmology, Mystics], Gefin, Taylor [Volume I], Godwin [Kircher], Kircher [*Oedipus Aegyptiacus*]

2.3 The Interpretation Process of Serial Images in the Consciousness

> **2.3.1 Interpretation of Ideogrammic Streams**—Clement, Gelb, Gefin
> **2.3.2 Interpretation of The Ideogrammic Streams of Dreams**—Khaldun, Silver
> **2.3.3 Analogy as the Agent of Imagination**—Silver

Chapter 3. Egyptian Hieroglyphic Imagery Depiction of Thoughts

> **3.1 Ideograms of Ideas [Images as Metaphysical Symbols]**—Gadalla [Culture, Harmony], Silver, Plotinus [Armstrong], Iverson, Gefin, Taylor [*Volume I*]
> **3.2 An Overview of the Egyptian Application of Ideograms**
>
>> **3.2.1 The Wealth of Knowledge in the Egyptian Pictorial Formations**—Gadalla [Cosmology]
>> **3.2.2 Man Depiction Signifies the Universe**—Gadalla [Cosmology, Mystics, Harmony], Wilkinson [Reading & Symbol]
>> **3.2.3 Animal Symbolism**—Gadalla [Cosmology, Divinities], Wilkinson [Reading & Symbol]

3.2.4 Accessories, Emblems, Color, etc.—Gadalla [Cosmology], Wilkinson [Reading & Symbol]

3.2.5 Action Forms—Individual Hieroglyphics PLUS Sequence of Symbols—Gadalla [Harmony], Wilkinson [Reading & Symbol]

3.2.6 Orientations of Hieroglyphic Characters—Gardiner, Wilkinson [Reading & Symbol]

Chapter 4. Animal Hieroglyphic Images [Animal Symbolism]

4.1 Metaphysical Significance of Animal Images—Gardiner, Drucker, Wilkinson [Reading & Symbol], Gadalla [Culture]

4.2 Sample Related Egyptian Hieroglyphic Images

Ass—Gardiner, Wilkinson [Reading & Symbol], Gadalla [Cosmology & Divinities]

Ba—Gardiner, Wilkinson [Reading & Symbol], Gadalla [Cosmology]

Baboon—Gardiner, Wilkinson [Reading & Symbol], Gadalla [Divinities]

Baby Chick—Gardiner, Wilkinson [Reading & Symbol]

Bee—Gardiner, Wilkinson [Reading & Symbol]

Beetle—Gardiner, Wilkinson [Reading & Symbol], Horapollo, Gadalla [Cosmology & Divinities]

Birds—Gardiner, Wilkinson [Reading & Symbol], Gadalla [Culture]

Bulls—Gardiner, Wilkinson [Reading & Symbol], Gadalla [Cosmology & Divinities], Clement, Diodorus, Horapollo

Cat—Gardiner, Wilkinson [Reading & Symbol], Gadalla [Cosmology & Divinities]
Cows—Gardiner, Wilkinson [Reading & Symbol], Gadalla [Cosmology & Divinities]
Crocodile—Gardiner, Wilkinson [Reading & Symbol], Gadalla [Divinities & Christianity], Clement, Diodorus
Dogs—Gardiner, Wilkinson [Reading & Symbol], Gadalla [Cosmology, Culture, Mystics & Divinities], Clement
Egg—Gardiner, Wilkinson [Reading & Symbol], Gadalla [Divinities]
Falcons—Gardiner, Wilkinson [Reading & Symbol], Clement, Plutarch, Diodorus, Gadalla [Divinities]
Feather—Gardiner, Wilkinson [Reading & Symbol], Gadalla [Divinities]
Fish—Gardiner, Wilkinson [Reading & Symbol], Gadalla [Culure], Clement, Plutarch
Frog—Gardiner, Wilkinson [Reading & Symbol], Gadalla [Cosmology & Divinities]
Giraffe—Gardiner, Wilkinson [Reading & Symbol]
Goose—Gardiner, Wilkinson [Reading & Symbol], Gadalla [Divinities], Horapollo, Iverson
Hare—Gardiner, Wilkinson [Reading & Symbol]
Heron—Gardiner, Wilkinson [Reading & Symbol], Gadalla [Cosmology & Divinities]
Hippopotamus—Gardiner, Wilkinson [Reading & Symbol], Plutarch, Gadalla [Divinities]
Hoopoe—Gardiner, Wilkinson [Reading & Symbol], Gadalla [Cosmology]
Horse—Gardiner, Wilkinson [Reading & Sym-

bol], Clement, Gadalla [Cosmology]
Ibis—Gardiner, Wilkinson [Reading & Symbol], Clement, Plutarch, Gadalla [Harmony]
Lion & Lioness—Gardiner, Wilkinson [Reading & Symbol], Clement, Gadalla [Cosmology & Divinities]
Pig—Gardiner, Wilkinson [Reading & Symbol]
Rams—Gardiner, Wilkinson [Reading & Symbol], Gadalla [Cosmology & Divinities]
Serpents—Gardiner, Wilkinson [Reading & Symbol], Gadalla [Cosmology & Divinities]
Vulture—Gardiner, Wilkinson [Reading & Symbol], Gadalla [Cosmology & Divinities], Iverson, Horapollo

Chapter 5. Human and Animal-Headed Human Hieroglyphic Images

5.1 Metaphysical Significance of Human Images—Gadalla [Cosmology, Harmony & Divinities]
5.2 Metaphysical Significance of Animal Headed Images—Gadalla [Cosmology & Divinities]
5.3 Sample Related Egyptian Hieroglyphic Images—Drucker, Gadalla [Cosmology & Divinities]

Aged Man with Stick—Gardiner, Wilkinson [Reading & Symbol], Plutarch, Clement
Bound Arms—Gardiner, Wilkinson [Reading & Symbol]
Child—Inquiring—Gardiner, Wilkinson [Reading & Symbol], Clement, Gadalla [Divinities]
Man with a Stick—Wilkinson [Reading & Symbol]

Seated with No Seat—Gardiner, Wilkinson [Reading & Symbol], Gadalla [Cosmology]
Seated on a Seat—Wilkinson [Reading & Symbol], Gadalla [Cosmology]
Shepherd—Gardiner, Wilkinson [Reading & Symbol], Gadalla [Cosmology & Divinities]
Woman and Child—Gardiner, Wilkinson [Reading & Symbol], Gadalla [Cosmology]

Chapter 6. Human Body Parts Hieroglyphic Images

6.1 Metaphysical Significance of Human Body Parts Images—Gadalla [Cosmology & Harmony]
6.2 Sample Related Egyptian Hieroglyphic Images—Drucker, Gadalla [Cosmology & Harmony]

Arms [incl. Ka & cubit]—Gardiner, Wilkinson [Reading & Symbol], Gadalla [Cosmology & Harmony]
Ears—Gardiner, Wilkinson [Reading & Symbol], Gadalla [Cosmology]
Eye & Its Parts—Gardiner, Wilkinson [Reading & Symbol], Diodorus, Gadalla [Cosmology & Harmony]
Female Genitalia—Gardiner, Wilkinson [Reading & Symbol], Gadalla [Cosmology & Divinities]
Hand and Fingers—Gardiner, Wilkinson [Reading & Symbol], Budge [Amulets], Gadalla [Cosmology], Diodorus, Sorell
Head—Gardiner, Wilkinson [Reading & Symbol], Gadalla [Cosmology]
Heart—Gardiner, Wilkinson [Reading & Symbol], Gadalla [Cosmology]

Legs—Gardiner, Wilkinson [Reading & Symbol]
Mouth—Gardiner, Wilkinson [Reading & Symbol], Gadalla [Cosmology, Divinities & Harmony]
Phallus—Gardiner, Wilkinson [Reading & Symbol], Gadalla [Cosmology]

Chapter 7. Nature and Geometrical Figures Hieroglyphic Images

7.1 Sample Related Egyptian Hieroglyphic Images—Drucker, Gadalla [Cosmology & Harmony]

Buds—Gardiner, Wilkinson [Reading & Symbol], Gadalla [Cosmology & Divinities]
Circle & Parts of [full—cross in full—top half—neb]—Gardiner, Wilkinson [Reading & Symbol], Gadalla [Cosmology, Divinities, Mystics & Harmony]
Sky/firmament—Gardiner, Wilkinson [Reading & Symbol], Gadalla [Cosmology & Divinities]
Spiral—Gardiner, Wilkinson [Reading & Symbol], Gadalla [Cosmology & Harmony]
Star—Gardiner, Wilkinson [Reading & Symbol], Horapollo, Gadalla [Cosmology & Harmony]
Sun and Moon [solar and lunar principles]—Diodorus, Gadalla [Cosmology & Divinities]
Triangles—Gardiner, Wilkinson [Reading & Symbol], Plutarch, Gadalla [Cosmology & Harmony]
Trees—Gardiner, Wilkinson [Reading & Symbol] Plutarch, *Book of Dead*, Kastor, Gadalla [Cos-

mology, Mystics & Divinities]
Water Surface [1 or 3]—Gardiner, Wilkinson [Reading & Symbol], Gadalla [Mystics]

Chapter 8. Man Made Object Hieroglyphic Images

8.1 Metaphysical Significance of Man Made Object Images—Gadalla [Cosmology & Harmony], Gefin
8.2 Sample Related Egyptian Hieroglyphic Images—Drucker, Gadalla [Cosmology & Harmony]

Ankh—Gardiner, Wilkinson [Reading & Symbol], Gadalla [Cosmology]
Ark—Gardiner, Wilkinson [Reading & Symbol], Gadalla [Mystics]
Ax—Gardiner, Wilkinson [Reading & Symbol], Gadalla [Cosmology]
Bed—Gardiner, Wilkinson [Reading & Symbol], Gadalla [Cosmology]
Crook—Gardiner, Wilkinson [Reading & Symbol], Gadalla [Cosmology]
Crowns—Gardiner, Wilkinson [Reading & Symbol], Gadalla [Cosmology]
Farming Tools—Gardiner, Wilkinson [Reading & Symbol], Gadalla [Cosmology]
Flail—Gardiner, Wilkinson [Reading & Symbol], Gadalla [Cosmology]
Knife—Gardiner, Wilkinson [Reading & Symbol], Gadalla [Cosmology]
Knots Tying—Gardiner, Wilkinson [Reading & Symbol], Gadalla [Cosmology]
Ropes Twisted—Gardiner, Wilkinson [Reading & Symbol], Gadalla [Cosmology]
Scale—Gardiner, Wilkinson [Reading & Sym-

bol], Gadalla [Cosmology]
Scepter—Gardiner, Wilkinson [Reading & Symbol], Gadalla [Cosmology]
Seat—Gardiner, Wilkinson [Reading & Symbol], Gadalla [Cosmology, Divinities]
Tet Pillar—Gardiner, Wilkinson [Reading & Symbol], Gadalla [Cosmology]
Was Scepter—Gardiner, Wilkinson [Reading & Symbol], Gadalla [Cosmology]
Wine Press—Gardiner, Wilkinson [Reading & Symbol], Gadalla [Cosmology, Christianity]

TRF PUBLICATIONS

Tehuti Research Foundation (T.R.F.) is a non-profit, international organization, dedicated to Ancient Egyptian studies. Our books are engaging, factual, well researched, practical, interesting, and appealing to the general public. Visit our website at:

https://www.egypt-tehuti.org
E-mail address: info@egypt-tehuti.org

The publications listed below are authored by T.R.F. chairman,
Moustafa Gadalla.

The publications are divided into three categories:

[I] **Current Publications in English Language**
[II] **Earlier Available Editions in English Language**
[III] **Current Translated Publications in Non English Languages**[Chinese, Dutch, Egyptian(so-called "arabic"), French, German, Hindi, Italian, Japanese, Portuguese, Russian & Spanish]

[I] **Current Publications in English Language**

Please note that printed editions of all books listed below are to be found at www.amazon.com

The Untainted Egyptian Origin—Why Ancient Egypt Matters

ISBN-13(pdf): 978-1-931446-50-1
ISBN-13(e-book): 9781931446-66-2

This book is intended to provide a short concise overview of some aspects of the Ancient Egyptian civilization that can serve us well nowadays in our daily life no matter where we are in this world. The book covers matters such as self empowerment, improvements to present political, social, economical and environmental issues, recognition and implementations of harmonic principles in our works and actions, etc.

The Ancient Egyptian Culture Revealed, Expanded 2nd ed.

ISBN-13(pdf): 978-1-931446-66-2
ISBN-13(e-book): 978-1-931446-65-5
ISBN-13(pbk.): 978-1-931446-67-9

This new expanded edition reveals several aspects of the Ancient Egyptian culture, such as the very remote antiquities of Egypt; the Egyptian characteristics and religious beliefs and practices; their social/political system; their cosmic temples; the richness of their language; musical heritage and comprehensive sciences; their advanced medicine; their vibrant economy; excellent agricultural and manufactured products; their transportation system; and much more.

Isis : The Divine Female

ISBN-13(pdf): 978-1-931446-25-9
ISBN-13(e-book): 978-1-931446- 26-6
ISBN-13(pbk.): 978-1-931446-31-0

This book explains the divine female principle as the source of creation (both metaphysically and physically); the feminine dual nature of Isis with Nephthys; the relationship (and one-ness) of the female and male principles; the numerology of Isis and Osiris; Isis' role as the Virgin Mother; explanation of about twenty female deities as the manifestations of the feminine attributes; the role of Isis' ideology throughout the world; the allegory of Isis, Osiris and Horus; and much more. This book will fill both the mind with comprehensive information as well as the heart with the whole spectrum of emotions.

Egyptian Cosmology, The Animated Universe, *Expanded 3rd edition*

ISBN-13(pdf): 978-1-931446-44-0
ISBN-13(e-book): 978-1-931446-46-4
ISBN-13(pbk.): 978-1-931446-48-8

This new expanded edition surveys the applicability of Egyptian cosmological concepts to our modern understanding of the nature of the universe, creation, science, and philosophy. Egyptian cosmology is humanistic, coherent, comprehensive, consistent, logical, analytical, and rational. Discover the Egyptian concept of the universal energy matrix and the creation process accounts. Read about numerology, dualities,trinities, numerical significance of individual numbers thru the number ten; how the human being is related to the universe; the Egyptian astronomical consciousness; the earthly voyage; how the social and political structures were a reflection of the universe; the cosmic role of the pharaoh; and the interactions between earthly living and other realms; climbing the heavenly ladder to reunite with the Source; and more.

Egyptian Alphabetical Letters of Creation Cycle

ISBN-13(pdf): 978-1-931446-89-1
ISBN-13(e-book): 978-1-931446-88-4
ISBN-13(pbk.): 978-1-931446-87-7

This book focuses on the relationship between the sequence of the creation cycle and the Egyptian ABGD alphabets; the principles and principals of Creation; the cosmic manifestation of the Egyptian alphabet; the three primary phases of the creation cycle and their numerical values; and the creation theme of each of the three primary phases, as well as an individual analysis of each of the 28 ABGD alphabetical letters that covers each letter's role in the Creation Cycle, its sequence significance, its sound and writing form significance, its numerical significance, its names & meanings thereof, as well as its peculiar properties and its nature/impact/influence.

Egyptian Mystics: Seekers of the Way, Expanded 2nd ed.

ISBN-13(pdf): 978-1-931446-53-2
ISBN-13(e-book): 978-1-931446-54-9
ISBN-13(pbk.): 978-1-931446-55-6

This new expanded edition explains how Ancient Egypt is the origin of alchemy and present-day Sufism, and how the mystics of Egypt camouflage their practices with a thin layer of Islam. The book also explains the progression of the mystical Way towards enlightenment, with a coherent explanation of its fundamentals and practices. It includes details of basic training practices; samples of Ancient Present Egyptian festivals; the role of Isis as the 'Model Philosopher'.It shows the correspondence between the Ancient Egyptian calendar of events and the cosmic cycles of the universe; and other related miscellaneous items.

Egyptian Divinities: The All Who Are THE ONE, Expanded 2nd ed.

ISBN-13(pdf): 978-1-931446-57-0
ISBN-13(e-book): 978-1-931446-58-7
ISBN-13(pbk.): 978-1-931446-59-4

This new expanded edition shows how the Egyptian concept of God is based on recognizing the multiple attributes of the Divine. The book details more than 100 divinities (gods/goddesses); how they act and interact to maintain the universe; and how they operate in the human being—As Above so Below, and As Below so Above.It includes details of the manifestations of the neteru (gods, goddesses) in the creation process; narrations of their manifestations; man as the universal replica; the most common animals and birds neteru; and additional male and female deities.

The Ancient Egyptian Roots of Christianity, 2nd ed.

ISBN-13(pdf): 978-1-931446-75-4
ISBN-13(e-book): 978-1-931446-76-1
ISBN-13(pbk.): 978-1-931446-77-8

This new expanded edition reveals the Ancient Egyptian roots of Christianity, both historically and spiritually. This book demonstrates that the accounts of the "historical Jesus" are based entirely on the life and death of the Egyptian Pharaoh, Twt/Tut-Ankh-Amen; and that the "Jesus of Faith" and the Christian tenets are all Egyptian in origin—such as the essence of the teachings/message, as well as the religious holidays.It also demonstrates that the major biblical ancestors of the biblical Jesus—being David, Solomon and Moses are all Ancient Egyptian pharaohs as well as a comparison between the creation of the universe and man (according to the Book of Genesis) and the Ancient Egyptian creation accounts.

The Egyptian Pyramids Revisited, Expanded Third Edition

ISBN-13(pdf): 978-1-931446-79-2
ISBN-13(e-book): 978-1-931446-80-8
ISBN-13(pbk.): 978-1-931446-81-5

The new expanded edition provides complete information about the pyramids of Ancient Egypt in the Giza Plateau. It contains the locations and dimensions of interiors and exteriors of these pyramids; the history and builders of the pyramids; theories of construction; theories on their purpose and function; the sacred geometry that was incorporated into the design of the pyramids;

and much, much more. It also includes details of the interiors and exteriors of the Saqqara's Zoser Stepped "Pyramid" as well as the three Snefru Pyramids that were built prior to the Giza Pyramids. It also discusses the "Pyramid Texts" and the works of the great pharaohs who followed the pharaohs of the Pyramid Age.

The Ancient Egyptian Metaphysical Architecture, Expanded Edition

ISBN-13(pdf): 978-1-931446-63-1
ISBN-13(e-book): 978-1-931446-62-4
ISBN-13(pbk): 978-1-931446-61-7

This new expanded edition reveals the Ancient Egyptian knowledge of harmonic proportion, sacred geometry, and number mysticism as manifested in their texts, temples, tombs, art, hieroglyphs, etc., throughout their known history. It shows how the Egyptians designed their buildings to generate cosmic energy; and the mystical application of numbers in Egyptian works. The book explains in detail the harmonic proportion of about 20 Ancient Egyptian buildings throughout their recorded history.It also includes additional discussions and details of the symbolism on the walls; the interactions between humans and the divine forces; Egyptian tombs, shrines and housing; as well as several miscellaneous related items.

Sacred Geometry and Numerology,

ISBN-13(e-book): 978-1-931446-23-5

This document is an introductory course for learning the fundamentals of sacred geometry and numerology, in its true and complete form, as practiced in the Egyptian traditions.

The Egyptian Hieroglyph Metaphysical Language

ISBN-13(pdf): 978-1-931446-95-2
ISBN-13(e-book): 978-1-931446-96-9
ISBN-13(pbk.): 978-1-931446-97-6

This book covers the Egyptian Hieroglyph metaphysical language of images/pictures; the language of the mind/intellect/divine; the scientific/metaphysical realities of pictorial images (Hieroglyphs) as the ultimate medium for the human consciousness that interpret, process and maintain the meanings of such images; how each hieroglyphic image has imitative and symbolic (figurative and allegorical) meanings; the concurrence of modern science of such multiple meanings of each image; how Egyptian hieroglyphic images represent metaphysical concepts; and the metaphysical significance of a variety of about 80 Egyptian Hieroglyphic images.

The Ancient Egyptian Universal Writing Modes

ISBN-13(pdf): 978-1-931446-91-4
ISBN-13(e-book): 978-1-931446-92-1
ISBN-13(pbk.): 978-1-931446-93-8

This book will show how the Egyptians had various modes of writings for various purposes, and how the Egyptian modes were falsely designated as "separate languages" belonging to others; the falsehood of having different languages on the Rosetta (and numerous other similar) Stone; and evaluation of the "hieratic' and "demotic" forms of writing. The book will also highlight how the Egyptian alphabetical language is the MOTHER and origin of all languages (as confirmed by all writers of antiquities) and how this one original language came to be called Greek, Hebrew, Arabic and other 'languages' throughout the world through the deterioration of sound values via 'sound shifts', as well as foreign degradation of the original Egyptian writing forms.

The Enduring Ancient Egyptian Musical System—Theory and Practice, Expanded Second Edition

ISBN-13(pdf): 978-1-931446-69-3
ISBN-13(e-book): 978-1-931446-70-9
ISBN-13(pbk.): 978-1-931446-71-6

This new expanded edition explains the cosmic roots of Egyptian musical and vocal rhythmic forms. Learn the fundamentals (theory and practice) of music in the typical Egyptian way: simple, coherent, and comprehensive.It provides discussions and details of an inventory of Ancient Egyptian musical instruments explaining their ranges and playing techniques. It also discusses Egyptian rhythmic dancing and musical harmonic practices by the Ancient Egyptians and other miscellaneous items.

Egyptian Musical Instruments, 2nd ed.

ISBN-13(pdf): 978-1-931446-47-1

ISBN-13(e-book): 978-1-931446-73-0
ISBN-13(pbk.): 978-1-931446-74-7

This book presents the major Ancient Egyptian musical instruments, their ranges, and playing techniques.

***

The Musical Aspects of the Ancient Egyptian Vocalic Language

ISBN-13(pdf): 978-1-931446-83-9
ISBN-13(e-book): 978-1-931446-84-6
ISBN-13(pbk.): 978-1-931446-85-3

This book will show that the fundamentals, structure, formations, grammar, and syntax are exactly the same in music and in the Egyptian alphabetical language. The book will show the musical/tonal/tonic Egyptian alphabetical letters as being derived from the three primary tonal sounds/vowels; the fundamentals of generative phonology; and the nature of the four sound variations of each letter and their exact equivalence in musical notes; the generative nature of both the musical triads and its equivalence in the Egyptian trilateral stem verbs; utilization of alphabetical letters and the vocalic notations for both texts and musical instruments performance; and much more.

***

Egyptian Romany: The Essence of Hispania, *Expanded 2nd ed.*

ISBN-13(pdf.): 978-1-931446-43-3
ISBN-13(e-book): 978-1-931446- 90-7
ISBN-13(pbk.): 978-1-931446-94-5

This new expanded edition reveals the Ancient Egyptian roots of the Romany (Gypsies) and how they brought about the civilization and orientalization of Hispania over the past 6,000 years. The book shows also the intimate relationship between Egypt and Hispania archaeologically, historically, culturally, ethnologically, linguistically, etc. as a result of the immigration of the Egyptian Romany (Gypsies) to Iberia.It alsp provides discussions and details of the mining history of Iberia; the effects of Assyrians and Persians attacks on Ancient Egypt and the corresponding migrations to Iberia; the overrated "Romans" influence in Iberia; and other miscellaneous items.

[II] Earlier Available Editions in English Language — continue to be available in PDF Format

Historical Deception: The Untold Story of Ancient Egypt, 2nd ed.

ISBN-13: 978-1-931446- 09-1

Reveals the ingrained prejudices against Ancient Egypt from major religious groups and Western academicians.

Tut-Ankh-Amen: The Living Image of the Lord

ISBN-13: 978-1-931446- 12-1

The identification of the "historical Jesus" as that of the Egyptian Pharaoh, Twt/Tut-Ankh-Amen.

Exiled Egyptians: The Heart of Africa

ISBN-13: 978-1-931446-10-5

A concise and comprehensive historical account of Egypt and sub-Sahara Africa for the last 3,000 years.

The Twilight of Egypt

ISBN-13: 978-1-931446-24-2

A concise and comprehensive historical account of Egypt and the Egyptians for the last 3,000 years.

[III] Current Translated Publications in Non English Languages [Chinese, Dutch, Egyptian (so-called "arabic"), French, German, Hindi, Italian, Japanese, Portuguese, Russian & Spanish]

Details of All Translated Publications are to be found on our website

Printed in Great Britain
by Amazon